All the Way Home

A DRAMA IN THREE ACTS

By Tad Mosel

Based on the Pulitzer Prize Novel
"*A Death in the Family*," by James Agee.
Pulitzer Prize Play, 1961
Winner New York Critics' Award, 1961

SAMUEL FRENCH, INC.
45 WEST 25TH STREET   NEW YORK 10010
7623 SUNSET BOULEVARD   HOLLYWOOD 90046
LONDON   *TORONTO*

The premiere performance of ALL THE WAY HOME was presented on November 30, 1960 at the Belasco Theatre by Fred Coe in association with Arthur Cantor. A new play by Tad Mosel, it was based on the Pulitzer Prize novel, "A Death in the Family," by James Agee.

CHARACTERS
(In order of appearance in the play)

RUFUS FOLLET	*John Megna*
BOYS	*Larry Provost*
	Jeff Conaway
	Gary Morgan
	Robert Ader
JAY FOLLET	*Arthur Hill*
MARY FOLLET	*Colleen Dewhurst*
RALPH FOLLET	*Clifton James*
SALLY FOLLET	*Lenka Peterson*
JOHN HENRY FOLLET	*Edwin Wolfe*
JESSIE FOLLET	*Georgia Simmons*
JIM-WILSON	*Christopher Month*
AUNT SADIE FOLLET	*Dorrit Kelton*
GREAT-GREAT-GRANMAW	*Lylah Tiffany*
CATHERINE LYNCH	*Lillian Gish*
AUNT HANNAH LYNCH	*Aline MacMahon*
JOEL LYNCH	*Thomas Chalmers*
ANDREW LYNCH	*Tom Wheatley*
FATHER JACKSON	*Art Smith*

The action takes place in and around Knoxville, Tenn., in May of 1915.

ACT ONE
The first day.

ACT TWO
The second day.

ACT THREE
Two days later

All the Way Home

ACT ONE

AT RISE: RUFUS, *aged six, Down Right. Three older* BOYS *wearing rakish gawdy caps dance around him, jumping up and down with ferocious joy, shoving their fingers at his chest, his stomach and face, screaming and chanting.* JAY *watches, Down Left, unseen by them.*

RUFUS. (*As the Curtain rises, one clear frantic call.*) My name is Rufus!

THREE BOYS (*Together.*) Nigger's name, nigger's name, nigger's name!

RUFUS. Rufus! Rufus!

FIRST BOY. (*As the others chant "Nigger's Name!"*)
      Nigger, nigger, black as tar,
      Tried to ride a 'lectric car,
      Car broke down and broke his back,
      Poor nigger wanted his nickel back!

RUFUS. I'm Rufus!

THREE BOYS. (*Together.*)
    Uh-Rufus, uh-Rastus, uh-Johnson, uh-Brown,
    Uh-what ya gonna do when the rent come 'roun'?
    Uh-Rufus, uh-Rastus, uh-Johnson, uh-Brown,
    Uh-what ya gonna do when the rent comes 'roun'?

(RUFUS *makes one desperate effort to escape, running straight into* JAY'S *arms.*)

FIRST BOY. Nigger name! Hey, we're gonna catch hell!

(*They scramble off, and* JAY *looks after them, glowering. Then he puts his hand on* RUFUS'S *head and smiles down at him.*)

JAY. What in the world you doin', Google Eyes?

RUFUS. I wish my name was Google Eyes.

JAY. No you don't, because that's a funny name. You wouldn't want to be called by a funny name.

RUFUS. Rufus is a funny name.

JAY. No, honey, it ain't.

RUFUS. It's a nigger's name.

JAY. (*Looking out over the valley.*) Look, we got a nice clear day for the outing, don't we? You can see all the way to North Knoxville. And if you squint your eyes you can see the North Pole. Squint your eyes. (*They* BOTH *squint for a moment.*) See the Pole? (RUFUS *nods, enchanted.*) And see that puff o' smoke comin' up over the hill? That means there'll be a train along the viaduct any minute. The one-oh-seven.

MARY. (*Off.*) Rufus—?

RUFUS. Mama's calling me.

JAY. (*Taking his hand, in high good spirits.*) Let's just watch that train go by! (*They* BOTH *look out.*) You know, Rufus is a very fine old name, Rufus. Some colored people take it too, but that is perfectly all right and nothing for them to be ashamed of, or for white people to be ashamed of who take it. You were given that name because it was your Great-Grandfather Lynch's name, your mama's grandfather, and it's a name to be proud of. You're proud of it, ain't you?

RUFUS. Yes, sir.

JAY. Then you got to stand up for it. Can you spell brave?

RUFUS. B-r-a-v-e.

JAY. Now proud.

RUFUS. P-r-o-u-d.

JAY. That's the one. Just keep spellin' that.

RUFUS. P-r-o-u-d.

JAY. You know what I'm proud of?

RUFUS. (*Guessing.*) Mama?

JAY. You, too. Why you're only six years old, and you can read and spell like I couldn't when I was twicet your age.

RUFUS. I wish you could be proud of me because I'm brave.

6

JAY. One of these days you'll get those boys to shake you by the hand. When a man shakes you by the hand, that means you've won him over. (*He puts out his hand.* RUFUS *grabs it.*) Hold on there, y'only got me by the ends of the fingers. Push your thumb clear up against mine, that's it!—then wrap your fingers as far's you can around the palm of my hand, right to the other side, if you can. Now squeeze. Not too much, that's just braggin'. Just enough to show you mean what you're doin'. Now shake. (*They solemnly shake, and* JAY *looks off excitedly.*) There she goes, right on time! (*With a burst of good spirits, he begins to sing.*)

> "Oh, I hear them train cars a-rumblin',
> And, they're mighty near at hand,
> I hear that train car a-rumblin',
> Come a-rumblin' through the land!"

(*He lifts* RUFUS *to his shoulders.*)

> "Git on board, little children,
> Git on board, little children,
> Git on board, little children,
> There's room for many and more!"

(*As he sings, the LIGHTS come up on the house.* MARY FOLLET *is placing bowls of flowers in the living room.*)

> "Oh, I look a way down yonder,
> And, uh-what do you reckon I see,
> A-band of shinin' angels
> A-comin' after me!"

(MARY *joins in the chorus, and they achieve some pleasing harmonies.*)

JAY *and* MARY. (*Singing.*)
> "Git on board, little children,
> Git on board, little children,
> Git on board, little children,
> There's room for many and more!"

(MARY *has come down to them, and as they finish the song,* JAY *swings* RUFUS *lightly to the ground.*)

RUFUS. Here comes the one-oh-seven! (*He chugs into the house like a train and settles into the Morris chair with his coloring book.*)

MARY. Don't you go away, Rufus! Your daddy's *people* will be here any minute! (*Turning to* JAY, *as if with a very amusing confidence she has been saving for him.*) Ralph just called up on the telephone!

JAY. Where from?

MARY. You know Ralph! He wasn't ten blocks away, just downtown. But instead of coming right on, he went to all the trouble of parking the machine, going in some place and calling up to say they were *almost* here! (*She laughs and places the tray on the ground beside the swing.*)

JAY. (*Laughing with her.*) Did you ever know anyone to get such a kick outa telephones?

MARY. If you ask me, he was in a saloon. Probably didn't want to telephone at all, if you know what I mean, but used it as an excuse to Sally for stopping, and then once he was in there he felt he'd better *really* call us, because Sally'd find out from us if he didn't and then she'd know that wasn't why he stopped!

JAY. (*Whistling.*) You sure can complicate a thought, Mama!

MARY. You know what I mean!

JAY. (*Grinning.*) Did he say anything about knockin' Kaiser Wilhelm's block off?

MARY. No. thank goodness, he was *very pleasant!* (*She laughs.*)

JAY. Then I reckon we'll still have a nice day.

MARY. (*Seriously.*) When they get here, Jay, you won't—I mean you won't let Ralph influence you?

JAY. Oh, I might hoist a few with him!

MARY. (*Uncertainly.*) Jay—?

JAY. Sure, you and the others go on to Great-Granmaw's! I figure Ralph and I'll stay here and have ourselves a bender! I'm just ripe for it!

MARY. Don't say that, even in fun!

JAY. (*Laughing, putting his arms around her.*) Aw now, Mary, you don't ever worry about me any more, do you?

MARY. I just don't like jokes about that particular subject.

JAY. And you know what I don't like? Super-intendents! No, sir, I don't like people lookin' down on me, thinkin' they got to keep an eye on me.

MARY. (*Shocked.*) Was I looking down on you?

JAY. Why, you was about ten feet off the ground!

MARY. (*Crushed.*) Honestly, Jay?

JAY. Two feet.

MARY. Well, *shame* on me. And I *certainly* thank you for pointing it out.

JAY. (*Impulsively holding her close, singing in her ear.*)

"I got a gal and a sugar babe, too—
    My honey, my darling . . ."

MARY. That awful song! (*She laughs.*)

JAY. I guess I know how to get on the good side of you, don't I?

MARY. I guess you do! (*He kisses her. She steps back primly, really tremendously pleased.*) Well, I certainly hope the neighbors enjoyed that! (*And she turns briskly into the living room.*) Rufus, I had this room all straightened up for your daddy's *people!*

JAY. (*Following.*) They won't be coming in here, Mary.

MARY. I want them to be able to if they want to, don't I?

JAY. (*Scraping his pipe into the ash tray.*) Rufus'll clean up the mess he made, won't you, honey?

MARY. And will *you* clean up the mess *you're* making with that pipe? Honestly, Jay! (*She is putting his law books into hall closet.*)

JAY. (*Picking up the dirtied ash tray, looking around, not knowing what to do with it.*) Rufus, did you ever think of starting a collection of pipe scrapelings?

RUFUS. (*At once interested.*) Scrapelings?

JAY. Sure, that's what they're called.

MARY. Really, Jay!

JAY. You wrap 'em up in a little piece of paper and you mark 'em with the date and whose pipe they come out of, then you put 'em away in some secret hiding place where no one'll ever find 'em.

MARY. (*Laughing.*) All *right*, Jay!

RUFUS. Please, Mama, may I?

MARY. Of course you may, just don't spill them all over everything! And get your feet off your daddy's chair—! (*She stoops to pick up the coloring book.*)

JAY. Rufus, don't make your mama pick up after·you—

MARY. (*Straightening up quickly.*) Oh—!

JAY. What is it, honey?

MARY. It just made me dizzy for a moment—

JAY. Here, you sit right down.

RUFUS. What's the matter, Mama?

JAY. Are you all right now?

MARY. Of course I am. It was just a thing of the minute. It's to be expected from now on.

RUFUS. (*Demanding.*) What's the *matter?*

MARY. Mama just stopped over very quickly, that's all, and it made the room go around.

RUFUS. (*Stoops over very quickly and straightens up hopefully.*) It's not going around.

MARY. Not for *you*, dear—

(MARY *and* RUFUS *are picking up his crayons and coloring book.*)

JAY. Why don't you tell him, Mary?

MARY. Oh Jay, please—!

RUFUS. Tell me what?

MARY. There, you *see?*

JAY. He has to find out some time.

MARY. But not *now*—!

RUFUS. Find out what, Mama?

JAY. Won't be long before he sees for himself that *some*thing's happening.

MARY. (*Flaring.*) Not if you don't bring it to his attention!

JAY. I'd have told him weeks ago if you'd let me!

MARY. I wanted to talk to Father Jackson first.

JAY. You don't need any priest to tell you how to talk to your own boy.

MARY. Jay, I don't want him asking q-u-e-s-t-i-o-n-s!

JAY. That won't do y'any good, Mama, he can out-spell the both of us put together.

RUFUS. (*He has been looking from one to the other during this. There is now a silence.*) I can get dizzy on a swing! Or if I turn around in circles fast like this—! (*He whirls.*) Look, Mama, *I'm* gettin' dizzy! Look!

MARY. Rufus. (*He stops whirling.*) Come here to Mama. (*She takes him on her lap.*) Rufus—after a while you're going to have a wonderful surprise.

RUFUS. Like a present?

MARY. Something. Only very much nicer.

RUFUS. What's it going to *be?*

MARY. If I told you, it wouldn't be a surprise any more, would it? (JAY *begins to frown.*)

RUFUS. Will I get it today?

MARY. No dear, not for a long time yet.

RUFUS. When summer vacation starts?

MARY. Not till after summer vacation *ends,* and you've gone back to school. Not even till after you've cut out your pumpkin for Hallowe'en.

RUFUS. Where is it now?

MARY. It's in heaven. Still up in heaven.

JAY. Tell him it's right here with us.

RUFUS. Right *here—*

JAY. (*Squatting before* RUFUS.) For the next few months, Rufus, you and I've got to take special care of Mama. (*He cups his hands as if holding a very fragile object.*) We've got to treat her like something that might just break. (RUFUS *lcoks wonderingly into the cup of* JAY'S *hands.*)

MARY. I think we've told him enough for the time being. He knows there's a surprise coming for us from heaven, and he has something to look forward to.

JAY. If we don't tell him all of it, honey, the older boys will in the streets. Would you like that?

RUFUS. (*Astounded.*) What do *they* know?

MARY. Nothing, dear, nothing at all!

11

RUFUS. (*Excitedly.*) Is it a cap, Mama? Is the surprise a cap?

MARY. (*Finding an outlet for her irritation.*) Rufus, I've told you again and again you can't *have* one of those cheap flashy caps! And I've told you to stay away from those rowdy boys!

JAY. What if *they* won't stay away from *him?*

MARY. (*Hugging* RUFUS.) Now darling, will you do Mama a favor? There's a lunch hamper on the kitchen table, and I want you to take it out by the alley so it'll be all ready to put in Uncle Ralph's car. Will you do that?

RUFUS. Do I have to?

JAY. Do what your mama says, Rufus. (*During the following,* RUFUS *struggles off with the hamper. There is an uncomfortable silence between* MARY *and* JAY.) I think it'd make him feel more grown-up if he had a cap like the older boys.

MARY. He's not grown-up, Jay.

JAY. It's kind of hard for a fellow to know where he stands around here. You tell him to stay away from the older boys, and I tell him to win 'em over. You say the surprise is up in the sky some place, I say it's right here on earth. Yes sir, it sure is hard for a fellow to know what's going on.

MARY. He's just a *child.*

JAY. All that about priests and *heaven*—! Sets my teeth on edge.

MARY. Oh Jay, sometimes I pray—

JAY. That's your privilege.

MARY. Now I can't say what I was going to say.

JAY. I'm listening.

MARY. But you're keeping your distance. As you always do when these things come up. There's a space of about a hundred miles between us.

JAY. And you've got that pursed-*up* look. That preachy pursed-up look.

(*Another awkward silence. Neither one gives in. Finally she goes to him.*)

MARY. When the baby comes, it'll be time enough for him to hear about it, Jay. (*She puts her arms around his waist and leans against him. He does not respond.*)

JAY. Sure, Mary.

MARY. (*Stepping back, hurt, starting for the kitchen.*) I thought we'd all have a glass of something cold before we start. (*He bangs his pipe loudly into the ashtray while she gets the lemonade pitcher from the icebox. She stops in the middle of the kitchen and closes her eyes.*) Oh Lord, in Thy mercy, who can do all things, close this gulf between us. Make us one in *Thee* as we are in earthly wedlock. For Jesus' sake, Amen. (*She crosses herself.* JAY *has followed and heard. She turns and sees him looking at her. There is a sudden loud whooping, off, and* RUFUS *runs in.*)

RUFUS. They're here, they're here! (*He tugs at his* FATHER *to get him outside, then runs off again.*)

MARY. That's not Ralph's car!

JAY. (*Laughing.*) But that sure is Ralph gettin' out! (*He hurries excitedly to the yard to meet* RALPH FOL-LET, *his brother.*) Hey there, Ralph!

RALPH. We made it, Jay, safe and sound!

JAY. (*Eagerly.*) Where'd you get the car?

RALPH. D'you like 'er?

JAY. (*Impressed.*) Chalmers, ain't it?

RALPH. Goes like sixty, Jay!

JAY. (*Laughing.*) What're you tryin' t' do, make me look like a piker?

RALPH. (*Punching at him.*) Well, y'are a piker, ya piker, with your old Tin Lizzy! (*Dashing to* MARY, *who has come out with a pitcher of lemonade.*) How ya been, sweetheart!

MARY. I'm fine, Ralph!

RALPH. (*Admiringly.*) I gotta hug ya, just gotta hug ya! (*He grabs her.*) You can hug Sally if you want to, Jay! *Ever'*body hugs *my* wife!

MARY. (*Pulls away from his whiskey breath.*) I thought we'd have a glass of something cold before we start, Ralph!

RALPH. Did I do somethin' wrong, Mary?

MARY. Goodness sakes, *no!* Just tell the rest of them

13

to get out of the car before they suffocate! (*Gestures to* JAY *that* RALPH's *breath is powerful*.)

RALPH. (*Yelling*.) Come on, ever'body, Mary's got us a glass of somethin' cold! And isn't it just like you, Mary! I was sayin' to them as we were drivin' along, I'll bet Jay's wife thinks of havin' somethin' cold waitin'—

RUFUS. (*He runs in crying*.) Daddy, Daddy—!

JAY. Why, what's the trouble, honey? (*Squatting to* RUFUS's *level*.) What you cryin' about? Wuzza matter, honey? (*He takes out his handkerchief*.)

RALPH. Oh, Jay, y'oughtn't ever to call a boy "honey"!

JAY. (*To* RUFUS.) Come on, blow. You know your mama don't like you to swallah that stuff.

MARY. What is it, Rufus, what's happened? (RUFUS *hides from her*.)

JAY. I reckon it ain't fit for ladies' ears, Mary. Maybe you better turn your back.

MARY. (*Turning away*.) Oh, for goodness *sakes!*

JAY. Now *tell* Daddy. (RUFUS *whispers in his ear*.) Is that all? Why, is that all it is?

MARY. What is it, Jay?

JAY. (*Standing, as* RUFUS *hides his face in shame*.) It seems that Rufus, here, has had a little accident.

MARY. Accident—?

RALPH. Did my Jim-Wilson hit him? Because if he did—

JAY. No, Ralph, nothin' like that. You know, Mary. An accident.

MARY. Oh, Rufus, you're too *old* for that! And I had you all dressed up for your daddy's people. Jay, you'll have to help him change.

JAY. He's old enough to manage by himself.

RALPH. (*With a whoop of delight*.) *That* kind of an accident?

JAY. Musta been the excitement of the day.

RALPH. Oh, that's rich, that is! (*In a sing-song*.) Rufus is a baby, Rufus is a baby! (RUFUS *runs into the house*.)

JAY. That'll do, Ralph!

RALPH. (*Laughing happily as* SALLY, JIM-WILSON, JESSIE *and* JOHN HENRY *come in from the car*. JESSIE

14

carries a small rubber inner tube.) Did y'hear that, ever'-body? Rufus had an accident! That's how my Chalmers affects people, they take one look at it and wet their britches!

SALLY. Ralph!

RALPH. Pee their pants!

(*There is sudden loud activity as EVERYBODY greets one another.*)

SALLY. (*To* MARY.) I think I'll take him right inside, Mary, and get it over with— (*She and* JIM-WILSON *start for the house.*)

MARY. You'll find everything ready for you, Sally, make yourself at home— Mother Follet; how good to see you!

RALPH. (*Simultaneously with above.*) Find a chair for Paw to sit down, Jay, he shouldn't stand around too much—this is what I like, all the Follets in one yard—where you goin', Sally?

JESSIE. (*To* MARY, *simultaneously with above.*) I reckon I'll just never get used to ridin' in automobiles, Mary, m'ear's all plugged up—not that Ralph ain't a good driver—

JAY. (*Simultaneously with above.*) You sit down right over here, Paw, and rest yourself—

RALPH. (*Shouting.*) Sally! (*All talking, greeting and movement stop.*) I asked you where you were goin'!

SALLY. I'm taking Jim-Wilson to the bathroom before we have any more accidents.

RALPH. Oh. Well, I just like you to answer me when I ask you a question! (SALLY *and* JIM-WILSON *continue on, with* RALPH *following as far as the kitchen.*) Did you hear me, Sally? I just like you to answer when I ask you a question! (*She is gone, and as the* OTHERS *talk in the yard,* RALPH *takes out a pint from his pocket and has a swallow.*)

JESSIE. Here, Paw, you better sit on your tube. (*She helps him to rise halfway and puts the inner tube underneath him.*)

15

MARY. Will you have something cold to drink, Mother Follet?

JESSIE. Wait on Paw first, if you will, Mary dear. I know how parched he gets. How's your breath, Paw?

JOHN HENRY. Pretty fair.

JAY. You haven't had any more of your attacks, have you, Paw?

JOHN HENRY. Not since that time last fall, Jay. (*He and* JESSIE *knock on the wood of their chairs.*)

JAY. (*Grinning.*) Maw sure does spoil you then.

JESSIE. When you come close to losing someone, that's the way you do.

JAY. Some easy life, I'll say!

JESSIE. I'm sure Mary spoils you enough.

MARY. (*Serving.*) Oh no, I think Jay spoils me!

JESSIE. So he should with another baby on the way. (*Eyeing her appraisingly.*) It don't show yet, do it, Mary? (MARY *laughs, embarrassed, and smooths her dress.*) Well, some show early, some show late. Ralph showed almost afore I knew he was there. Jay, you was a kicker. You all right, Paw?

JOHN HENRY. Pretty good.

MARY. (*Calling, as she returns to the tray of glasses.*) Ralph, are you in there?

RALPH. (*In the kitchen, quickly putting the bottle into his pocket.*) Be right with yuh, Mary!

MARY. Do you want some lemonade?

RALPH. (*Bustling out bringing with him bench from hall which will serve as front seat of his car.*) Thank yuh, Mary, I'm dry's a bone. (MARY *serves them lemonade.*)

JAY. Things must be pretty good for you, Ralph, if you can afford to go out and buy a new Chalmers.

RALPH. Oh yes, Jay, considerin' the state of the world 'n all, Ralph Follet's doin' fine, just fine!

JESSIE. (*Shaking her head.*) Tst, tst.

RALPH. Aw right, Maw, so I borrowed the money, but in this day and age you got to be in a sound financial situation to borrow money! (*Turning to* JAY *enthusiastically.*) Why, Jay, I walked into Ed Briggs' office at the bank in LaFollette, and he says "You want to buy a car,

16

Ralph? Take whatever you need!" That's how highly thought of I am in *that* bank!

JAY. I'm surprised he didn't give you the keys to the safe, Ralph.

RALPH. (*To his* PARENTS, *gratified.*) You hear what Jay said?

JOHN HENRY. I reckon Ed Briggs knew what he was doin'. An undertaker's always a good risk.

RALPH. It wasn't that, Paw!

JOHN HENRY. (*Bewildered.*) I'm tryin' to give you a compliment, son.

JESSIE. Paw's right. Only thing you can be sure of in life is, people go on dyin'.

MARY. Oh, Mother Follet, I'd rather say they go on being born.

JESSIE. (*Nodding.*) That too, Mary, they got to be born afore they can die.

RALPH. Ed Briggs give me that money because it was *me* askin' for it! Why there's other undertakers in La-Follette he wouldn't give the time o' day to!

JESSIE. Just the same, your paw never owed a cent in his life, Ralph, did you, Paw? (SALLY *comes out.*)

JOHN HENRY. I'm even thinkin' maybe the farm'll be free and clear afore I die, Jay.

JAY. You worked hard for it, Paw.

JOHN HENRY. (*Vaguely.*) *You* owe any money, Jay?

RALPH. (*Before* JAY *can answer.*) What if he don't, *I* happen to want to give *Sally* some of life's refinements! I don't like the idea *my* wife ridin' around town in some old Tin Lizzy!

MARY. (*Laughing.*) Why, Ralph, I just love our Ford!

SALLY. I never get to ride around town in *any*thing! *He's* always off some place! He only bought that new car because of you, Jay, so he'd have a better one than yours, and don't let him tell you different!

MARY. I'm certainly anxious to *ride* in it! Aren't you, Jay?

JAY. (*Grinning at her.*) Just can't wait!

RALPH. (*Angrily to* SALLY.) And what're *you* doin' at home while I'm out in the car on *business,* just tell me that!

17

MARY. Why don't we get started! (*Calling.*) Rufus—?

RALPH. The trouble with my wife is she don't appreciate how I try to please her! (*To* SALLY.) You ask Maw the things she's had to do without all her life and see how lucky y'are!

JESSIE. Now I know one thing I *can* do without, and that's any more of this talk.

JAY. Sure, Ralph, come on! We've all been lookin' forward to a good time today!

RALPH. (*Sulking.*) I'm *havin'* a good time. (*As* JIM-WILSON *comes out; snapping at him.*) Get out here, Jim-Wilson, and start enjoyin' yourself.

SALLY. (*To* JIM-WILSON.) Would you like some lemonade, dear?

RALPH. My God, she just gets him all drained out and she fills him up again!

MARY. Did you see Rufus in there, Jim-Wilson?

RALPH. (*Sing-song.*) Rufus is a baby, Rufus is a baby!

MARY. Please, Ralph, that's enough of that.

RALPH. Rufus is a ba-by!

MARY. Ralph, you're to stop!

RALPH. Just teasin', Mary!

MARY. Well, you're to stop it, what*ever* it is! The child had a perfectly normal accident!

RALPH. Why, Jim-Wilson hasn't had an accident like that in years, and he's younger'n Rufus by 'leven months!

MARY. (*Angrily.*) I don't care what Jim-Wilson does! (*Catching herself.*) I didn't mean that, of course, Sally. (*Stooping quickly to hug* JIM-WILSON.) Aunt Mary cares the *world* about Jim-Wilson!

RALPH. (*Laughing.*) God-damn it, why is it ever'-thin' I say today gets me into trouble!

MARY. And I'll thank you not to take the Lord's name in vain.

RALPH. This family ain't Catholic and I'll take the Lord's name any way that comes to mind.

JESSIE. Tst, tst.

JAY. You sure like to hit all bases, don't you, Ralph.

RALPH. I'm sorry for what I said, Jay. Mary, Jim-Wilson does pee his pants every day without fail.

JAY. Then I think you oughta get Rufus out here and apologize to him for making fun of him.

RALPH. Sure, Jay, of course. (*Calling.*) Rufus—? Come on out there, Rufus. (RUFUS *steals down the stairs from his room.*) This is your Uncle Ralph callin' to you. I promise not t' tease y'any more. D'you hear me, Rufus? (RUFUS *comes out.*) There he is. Looky here. (*He digs into his pocket and pulls out a business card.*) I got somethin' for you. Take it. "Ralph Follet, Mortician." We friends again? (RUFUS *looks to* JAY *who pantomimes shaking hands.* RUFUS *puts out his hand and* RALPH *shakes it, pretending to writhe in the strength of* RUFUS' *grip.*) Oh-o-o-ooh! That's what I like, ever'body friends again. All the Follets are friends, ain't we, Mary?

MARY. Of course we are, Ralph. (MARY *gathers up the glasses to take inside.* JESSIE *helps* JOHN HENRY *to rise, taking up the inner tube from the seat beneath him.*)

JESSIE. If we're goin' t'get there this afternoon, we'd best get started.

RALPH. Maw's right! Come on, ever'body, pile in the Chalmers! Jay, you and Mary sit up front with me, and Rufus—you can sit on my lap, Rufus, and maybe I'll even let you *steer—! (He has picked up* RUFUS *and held him high in the air.*)

SALLY. I think Jay ought to drive. (*It rings clearly through the happy activity, and all movement stops as EVERYBODY looks to* RALPH.)

RALPH. (*Incredulous, dropping* RUFUS *to the ground.*) Drive *my* car—?

SALLY. You're in no fit condition to drive it.

RALPH. Well, nobody else is goin' to drive it, I'll tell you that! Not *my* car!

SALLY. Can we go in your car, Jay?

RALPH. His old Tin Lizzy? We couldn't even all get in it!

SALLY. I'd rather be a little crowded and have Jay drive.

RALPH. Jay this an' Jay that, ever'body always lookin' up to Jay, askin' *Jay's* advice, lettin' *Jay* do the drivin'!

19

Well, let me tell you, there's been times when you wouldn't ride with him neither! *He's* been hauled outa the gutter more times'n you can count *and* put in jail *and* worse!

SALLY. You go ahead in the Chalmers, Ralph, and the rest of us'll follow with Jay in his car.

RALPH. (*Beside himself.*) And you'll be sittin' up there next to him, I suppose, rubbin' legs with him! So it's *Jay* you're after now!

JAY. That thought never once came into Sally's head and you know it. So dry up!

RALPH. Don't think you're the only one she's after, either! Don't get no swelled head it's just you! It's any man with a flat belly, that's who it is! Any man at all, so long as his belly don't get in the way! (JAY *attempts to take his arm, but* RALPH *swings wildly at him.*) Goddamn your flat belly! (*He stumbles towards the house, turning back for only a moment.*) I've a good mind t'go over there an' punch that Kaiser Wilhelm in the nose! Then maybe the lotta ya'll treat me with a little respect! (*He goes into the kitchen and a deep sigh seems to pass among the* PEOPLE *in the yard. He takes out his pint and has a swallow.*)

JESSIE. Better let me make you comfortable again, Paw. (*She puts the inner tube under him.*)

SALLY. Every time he sets out to enjoy himself he—gets so unhappy.

MARY. I'll look after him, Jay. (*She starts for the house.*)

JAY. (*Stopping her.*) I reckon you've had to do enough of that kinda lookin' after people—for your time. (*He goes into the kitchen to find* RALPH *staring fixedly at his hands.* MARY *crosses to the swing with* RUFUS. *Then she joins* SALLY *on the swing.* RUFUS *and* JIM-WILSON *go to play in the yard behind them.*)

RALPH. Smell my hands, Jay, go ahead, smell 'em.

JAY. Now, there's nothin' on your hands, Ralph.

RALPH. Yes there is, Jay, it's that f'maldehyde. *I* can't smell it but ever'body else can. I scrub 'em and scrub 'em, and I can't ever get rid of that smell. Why, last night I went to the picture show, and I was sittin' there next t'this girl and she got up and moved. It was that smell, Jay, don't you think?

JAY. Go on, Ralph, you're the worst tail chaser in LaFollette!

RALPH. (*Angrily.*) It was 'at smell made her move, I tell yuh! It's terrible t'work with it ever' day of your life, and then even when you go out for a good time t'have it go along with yuh. The picture show was good though. Charlie. You like Charlie?

JAY. Sure do.

RALPH. Last night he put a bag of eggs in the seat of his pants and then sat on 'em. (*He pantomimes this and sits in chair R. of table.*)

JAY. Rufus and I seen that one.

RALPH. You 'n I like lotsa the same things, Jay, maybe we're more brothers than we seem.

JAY. I reckon people'd know we was brothers.

RALPH. Thank yuh for that. (*Taking up the bottle.*) Well, outside they're thinkin' he's been in there long enough for two drinks, and I've only had one. If that's what they're goin' to think, I might's well *have* two! (*He drinks.*)

JAY. You sure can hold it, Ralph.

RALPH. (*Pushing the bottle across the table to him.*) He'p yourself.

JAY. Ever'body's waitin' on us, Ralph!

RALPH. Go on, Jay, Mary can't see. I tell you what, I'll keep watch for yuh!

JAY. It ain't that. (*He shoves the bottle at RALPH who grabs it from him.*)

RALPH. So God-damned reformed, ain't you!

JAY. I'm just thinkin' of you. If you keep pullin' away at that bottle, it ain't goin' to last you through the day. And I know that feelin' when the bottle's empty and you ain't full.

RALPH. (*Close to tears.*) I want it to be empty, Jay. I'm no good when I'm like this. No good at all. I'm mean and I'm reckless. I'm not even real. *I wish this bottle was empty!*

JAY. (*After a short silence, JAY grabs the bottle from him, drinks the last of the whiskey and drops the bottle*

21

loudly into the trash can.) Empty. Now are you ready to go?

RALPH. How's it make you feel, Jay?

JAY. That little bit don't make me feel anything.

RALPH. If you had a lot?

JAY. Come on, Ralph, it's gettin' late. If we're going to get to Great-Granmaw's and back before dark, we got to start.

RALPH. I ain't movin' from this spot till you tell me how it makes you feel!

JAY. Well, if I had as much as you, Ralph, I'd go quiet. So quiet, Ralph, I could hear the tickin' of the earth. And I'd be young as ever I could remember, and nothin' bad had ever happened to me or ever would. I wouldn't dare talk to no one, of course, for fear they'd show me the lie. And after a while it'd get lonesome in there all by myself, and I'd go off like a fire-cracker. If you happened to be standin' by, you'd get a few powder burns, let me tell you.

RALPH. What made you change, Jay? Was it Mary's religion?

JAY. Mary's religion is her own.

RALPH. How'd you do it, then?

JAY. I made a vow to myself. I said if I ever get drunk again, I'll kill myself.

RALPH. Oh, Jay. That's a strong vow.

JAY. Couldn't afford to leave myself any loopholes.

RALPH. Don't y'ever get thirsty?

JAY. There's too many reasons why I don't want to kill myself.

RALPH. What reasons?

JAY. There's two of 'em right out in the yard. (*Grinning.*) As a matter of fact, two'n a half.

RUFUS. (*Outside.*) Daddy!

JAY. (*His patience beginning to go.*) Now come on, Ralph, I promised them an outing today! They been lookin' forward to it for weeks, and I'm not goin' to disappoint them!

RALPH. I got reasons out in the yard too, don't I, Jay?

JAY. (*Giving him a towel, briskly.*) Now wipe off your face. You worked yourself into a sweat.

22

RALPH. (*He wipes his face.*) I could take that vow of yours, couldn't I, Jay?

JAY. Nobody's goin' to try and stop you!

RALPH. I'm takin' that vow this minute! (*He stands up and straightens himself.*) Stand back! Or Jay, maybe I could just take a vow that if ever I get drunk again I'll take your vow.

JAY. You better think on it, Ralph, that's a pretty serious step!

RALPH. (*Enthusiastically.*) All right, Jay, I tell you what! I hereby take a vow—to think on it!

JAY. Good for you! (*They come outside.*) All set, everybody?

SALLY. Which car are we going in?

JAY. Why, the Chalmers, of course. I wouldn't pass up a chance to ride in a Chalmers!

RALPH. But I've asked Jay to do the drivin'! I'm going to ride on the running board!

SALLY. Oh, Ralph!

RALPH. I got to point out the route to Jay, because I'm the only one remembers how to get there!

(*They begin to arrange themselves on the two benches which vaguely represent the* Chalmers. SALLY *is on the Upstage end of the piano bench,* JESSIE *next to her,* JOHN HENRY *Downstage holding* RUFUS *on his lap.* JAY *is on the Downstage end of the front bench with* MARY *beside him, holding* JIM-WILSON *in her lap.* RALPH *stands above them on the "running board.")*

JESSIE. Be sure you do remember, Ralph. We don't want to get lost in those mountains.

JOHN HENRY. There used to be cats back in those mountains. We called 'em painters then, Rufus. That's the same as a panther.

JAY. They was around here when I was a boy, Paw. And there still is bear, they claim. (JIM-WILSON *whimpers.*) Don't you fret, Jim-Wilson, we ain't likely to see any.

23

MARY. When was the last time all of you saw Great-Granmaw?

RALPH. I was the last to see her! I come out one day about twenty years ago!

MARY. Twenty years! Why for goodness sake, Ralph, you certainly have a wonderful memory to find the way!

RALPH. (*Pleased.*) I've always had a pretty good memory.

MARY. Why, that's *remarkable!* How long since you came out here, Jay?

JAY. I'm a-studyin' it. Nearly thirteen years. The last time was just before I went to Panama.

MARY. Then *you* were the last one to see her!

RALPH. Wait a minute, seems to me I seen her since then!

JOHN HENRY. Are you sure that's the place, Ralph? That don't look like I remember it.

RALPH. Oh that's it all right! Why sure! Only we come up on it from behind!

MARY. She doesn't live there alone, does she?

JOHN HENRY. My sister Sadie give her life to her. She wouldn't come and live with any of us. I raised my family in this cabin, she said, I lived all my life from fourteen years on and I aim to die here. That must have been a good thirty-five, most a good forty years ago, Grampaw died.

(SADIE *has begun slowly to push* GREAT GRANMAW *in a home-made wheelchair from Upstage Right to Down Right apron.*)

MARY. Goodness' sakes, and she was an old woman then!

JAY. She's a hundred and three years old. Hundred and three or hundred and four, she never could remember for sure which. But she knows she wasn't born later than eighteen twelve. And she always reckoned it might of been eighteen eleven.

MARY. Do you know what she is, Rufus? She's Grampa Follet's grandmother!

JOHN HENRY. That's a fact, Rufus. Woulda never be-

24

lieved you'd hear *me* call nobody Granma, now would you?

RUFUS. No sir.

JOHN HENRY. Well, you're gonna!

RALPH. (*Picking* JIM-WILSON *up from* MARY's *lap.*) Are you listenin' to all this, Jim-Wilson?

JAY. She's an old, old lady.

RALPH. (*An echo, awed.*) Old.

(AUNT SADIE *comes to meet them, they all stand.*)

SADIE. Lord God. (*She looks from one to the other.*) Lord God.

JOHN HENRY. Howdy, Sadie.

SADIE. Howdy, John Henry.

JOHN HENRY. Thought maybe you wouldn'ta knowed us.

SADIE. I know'd you all the minute I laid eyes on you. Just couldn't believe it. Howdy, Jessie.

JESSIE. It's good to see you, Sadie.

JAY. Howdy, Aunt Sadie.

SADIE. Howdy, Jay. You Jay's brother?

RALPH. I'm Ralph, Aunt Sadie.

SADIE. Howdy, Ralph.

RALPH. That's my machine we come in. And this is my bride, Sally. (*Glancing shyly at* SALLY.) That's how I thinka her.

SADIE. (*Looking at* SALLY.) Pretty.

JAY. And this is Mary, Aunt Sadie. Mary, this is Aunt Sadie.

SADIE. I'm proud to know you. I figured it must be you. And Rufus.

MARY. (*To* RUFUS.) Say hello to Aunt Sadie.

RUFUS. Hello, Aunt Sadie.

RALPH. Jim-Wilson? Step up and kiss your Aunt Sadie and give her a hug. *This* is *my* boy, Aunt Sadie.

SADIE. (*Snorts and grabs* JIM-WILSON's *hand, scaring him back into* SALLY's *skirts. Then she stands back.*) Howdy!

JAY. How's Granmaw?

SADIE. Good's we got any right to expect. But don't

25

feel put out if she don't know none-a-yews. She mought and she mought not. Half the time she don't even know me.

RALPH. Poor old soul.

SADIE. So if I was you-all, I'd come up on her kind of easy. Bin a coon's age since she seen so many folks at oncet. Me either. Mought skeer her if you all come a-whoopin' up on her in a flock.

JAY. Whyn't you go see her the first, Paw? You're the eldest.

JOHN HENRY. Tain't me she wants to see. Hit's the younguns'd tickle her most.

SADIE. Reckon that's true, if she can take notice. (*To* JAY.) She shore like to cracked her heels when she heard *yore* boy was borned. Proud as Lucifer. 'Cause that was the first.

MARY. I know. Fifth generation that made.

RALPH. Sally and I lost a baby the year *before* Rufus was born. That *woulda* been the first.

SADIE. (*To* JAY.) She always seemed to take a shine to you.

JAY. I always did take a shine to her.

SADIE. Did you get her postcard?

JAY. What postcard?

SADIE. When yore boy was borned.

MARY. Why, no!

SADIE. She told me what to write on one a them postcards and put hit in the mail to both a yews and I done it. Didn't you never git it?

JAY. First I've heard tell of it.

MARY. What street did you send it to, Aunt Sadie? Because we moved just before Rufus was born—

SADIE. Never sent it to no street. Never knowed I needed to, Jay working for the Post Office.

JAY. Why, I quit working for the post office a long time back, Aunt Sadie. I'm in law now, for Mary's paw.

SADIE. Well, I reckon that's how come then. 'Cause I just sent it to "Post Office, Cristobal, Canal Zone, Panama." And I spelt it right, too, C-r-i—

MARY. Oh.

26

JAY. Aw—why, Aunt Sadie, I thought you'd a known. I been living in Knoxvul since before I was married even.

SADIE. (*Looking at him keenly, almost angrily, then nodding several times.*) Well, they might just as well put me out to grass. Let me lay down and give me both barls threw the head.

MARY. Why, Aunt Sadie.

SADIE. I knowed that like I knowed my own name and it plum slipped my mind.

MARY. Oh, what a shame.

SADIE. If I git like that, too, then who's a-goana look out for *her?*

RALPH. What did she say on the postcard, Aunt Sadie?

SADIE. Lemme figger. Bin so long ago. (*She thinks for a moment.*) "I bin borned again," she says. "Love, Great-Granmaw."

MARY. Born again. Why that's beautiful.

SADIE. Mebbe. I always figgered bein' borned oncet was enough. (*She goes to* GREAT-GRANMAW.) Granmaw, ya got company. (*The* OLD WOMAN *does not move.* SADIE *speaks loudly but does not shout.*) It's Jay and his wife and the others come up from Knoxvul to see you. (*The hands crawl in the lap and the face turns toward the* YOUNGER WOMAN. *A thin, dry cackling, but no words.*) She knows ye. Come on over, Jay. (JAY, MARY *and* RUFUS *advance slowly, shyly.*) I'll tell her about the resta yuns in a minute.

RALPH. (*Herding the* OTHERS *back further.*) Aunt Sadie'll tell her about us in a minute.

SADIE. Don't holler. It only skeers her. Just talk loud and plain right up next her ear.

MARY. I know. My mother is deaf.

JAY. (*Bending close to Granmaw's ear.*) Granmaw? (*He draws away a little where she can see him.* GRANMAW *looks straight into his eyes and her eyes and face never change.* JAY *leans forward again and gently kisses her on the mouth. Then he draws back again, smiling a little anxiously. He speaks into her ear.*) I'm Jay. John Henry's boy. (*The* OLD LADY's *hands crawl on her skirt. Her mouth opens and shuts, emitting the low dry croaking. But her eyes do not change.*)

SADIE. (*Quietly.*) I figure she knows you.

JAY. She can't talk any more, can she?

SADIE. Times she can. Times she can't. Ain't only so seldom call for talk, reckon she loses the hang of it. But I figger she knows ye and I'm tickled she does.

JAY. Come here, Rufus.

MARY. Go to him. (*She gives RUFUS a gentle push toward JAY.*)

JAY. Just call her Granmaw. Get right up to her ear like you do to Granmaw Lynch and say, "Granmaw, I'm Rufus."

RUFUS. (*He walks over to GRANMAW as quietly as if she is asleep. He stands on tiptoe and puts his mouth to her ear.*) Granmaw, I'm Rufus.

JAY. Come out where she can see you.

RUFUS. (*He draws back and stands still further on tiptoe, leaning across where she can see him.*) I'm Rufus. (*Suddenly the old eyes dart a little and look straight into his, not changing expression.*)

JAY. Tell her, "I'm Jay's boy Rufus."

RUFUS. I'm Jay's boy Rufus.

JAY. Now kiss her. (*RUFUS kisses her. Suddenly the OLD WOMAN's hands grip his arms and shoulders, drawing him closer, looking at him, almost glaring, and suddenly she is smiling so hard that her chin and nose almost touch, and her eyes fill with light and almost giggle with joy. And again the croaking gurgle, making shapes that are surely words but incomprehensible words, and she holds him even more tightly and cocks her head to one side. With sudden love, RUFUS kisses her again.*)

MARY. (*Whispering, frightened.*) Jay—!

JAY. Let them be. (*After a moment, SADIE gently disengages GRANMAW's hands from RUFUS's arms. RUFUS steps back with his PARENTS, and the three of them edge away toward the OTHERS. They are now a good distance from GRANMAW. Watching intently as SADIE bends over her. GRANMAW's face settles back into its former expression, as if nothing has taken place.*)

MARY. (*Hushed.*) Is she all right?

SADIE. All she knows is somethin's been took from her.

28

(*A silence, and in the silence, the LIGHTS dim on*
GRANMAW, *leaving the* FAMILY *gazing at empty
space.*)

JOHN HENRY. We won't none of us ever see Granmaw
again.

JAY. I wouldn't be surprised, Paw. (*He goes into the
house and up to* RUFUS' *room.*)

JOHN HENRY. The hand of death is comin' close to
this family.

(JIM-WILSON *whimpers.*)

RALPH. (*Reverently, as he puts the piano bench back
under the piano.*) Well—when her time comes, I'll be—
honored to 'ficiate. Free of charge. (RALPH, SALLY *and*
JIM-WILSON *leave Down Left.*)

RUFUS. Mama? Do you know what happened?

MARY. What, dear?

RUFUS. Great-great-granmaw had an accident. (MARY
looks down at him.) When I kissed her. (MARY *looks
away, close to tears.*) Isn't she too old for that? (MARY
takes his hand and leads him off.) Isn't she, Mama?

JESSIE. How's your breath, Paw?

JOHN HENRY. Pretty fair.

(*They exit and the LIGHTS dim.* JAY *has been singing
softly. Now the LIGHTS come up on him as he
stands by* RUFUS' *bed singing him to sleep with
"Sugar Babe." He holds a tattered cloth dog in his
hands.* MARY *has been changing into her nightgown
in the bathroom. As she goes upstairs, her voice
joins his in clear, graceful harmonies. And the
LIGHTS come up on their bedroom as she comes
upstairs in her nightgown. She pulls down the win-
dow-shade, brushes her hair, turns down the bed
and sits on it to braid her hair.* JAY *looks down at
Rufus' bed and speaks softly.*)

JAY. Sleep now, Google-Eyes? (*There is no answer.
He quietly leaves the room. The LIGHT fades there.
He joins* MARY.) Look what I found.

29

MARY. What, dear?

JAY. His ole dog, Jackie.

MARY. (*Taking it.*) Goodness sakes, where was it?

JAY. Back in a corner under the crib. I was scarin' the Boogee Man outa there.

MARY. The *crib!* Shame on *me!*

JAY. Poor ole Jackie.

MARY. Is Rufus asleep?

JAY. Yeah, he's asleep.

MARY. What was the matter with him?

JAY. Bad dream, I reckon. (*He starts to undo his necktie.*) Pore little ole Jackie, so lonesome and thrown away. Remember when I got him?

MARY. Of course I do. You took such pleasure in picking him out.

JAY. Little ole Jackie was bigger'n Rufus. And I had to explain. "It's a dog," I had to say. Only "dog" was too big a word in those days. I gave you too soon, Jackie. And here it is too late. Left behind with the baby crib. (*He picks up the toy from the bed.*)

MARY. I'm certainly glad we kept that crib. It'll save buying a new one.

JAY. (*Tossing the toy to the floor.*) Back to the corner with you, Jackie.

MARY. Don't leave it there, darling. (*He retrieves the dog.*) What is it, Jay?

JAY. Nothin'. (*He stands in the middle of the room, the dog in his hands. She waits.*) I reckon it's just seein' Great-Granmaw again and rememberin' the summers I had out there. And it's seein' Paw begin to shrink up, and watchin' Ralph. And it's feelin' Rufus growin' bigger, and singin' those sad ole songs. And findin' Jackie. It's just the day, Mary.

MARY. It's been a long one.

JAY. (*He pulls at the dog and a piece comes off in his hand.*) Jackie's ear come off. It's enough to make a man thirsty. (*Abruptly, grimly, he dashes Jackie to the floor and runs downstairs where he takes a whiskey bottle from the hall closet. MARY picks up her robe and hurries down to find him standing in the living room, staring at the bottle. He goes into the kitchen.*) How far we all come, Mary. How far we all come away from ourselves. So far, so much between, you can't even remember where you started or what you had in mind or where you thought you were goin'. All you know is you were headin' *some* place. (*He hefts the bottle, as if testing its weight.*) One way you do remember. (*He puts the bottle on the kitchen table.*) You have a boy or a girl of your own, and now and then you sing to them or hold them, and you know how they feel, and it's almost the same as if you were your own self again. Just think, Mary, my paw used to sing to me. And before my time, even before I was dreamed of in this world, his daddy or his mother used to sing to him, and away on back through the mountains, back past Great-Granmaw, away on back through the years, right on back to Adam, only nobody ever sang to Adam.

MARY. God did.

JAY. Maybe God did.

MARY. We're supposed to come away from ourselves, Jay. That's the whole point. We're supposed to come away to— (*She stops herself.*)

JAY. I know. To God.

MARY. (*She nods.*) I don't see how you can *feel* the way you do and not believe in Him.

JAY. We come from people, Mary, and in time they fall away from us, like Great-Granmaw. We give birth to others, and in time they *grow* away from us, like Rufus will. (*He picks up the bottle.*) When we're about eighty years old, you 'n me, all we'll have left is us. And that's what I believe in. (*He puts the bottle back in the closet.*) Maybe that's it. Maybe that's where we're heading—to each other. And the sad thing all our lives is the distance between us. But maybe if we keep goin' in the direction we think is right, maybe we can't ever get all the way there, but at least we can make that distance less'n it was. (*She goes to him and they embrace.*) You'll catch cold down here like that. Now wait'll I warm up the bed for you. (*He runs upstairs and rubs his hand swiftly between the sheets. She follows him and sits on the bed. He kneels before her, removes her slippers and warms her feet in his hands.*) When I was a youngster on the farm, on cold nights we all used to pile into one bed together. Finally I was too big for that, but I wasn't too big to cry at bein' left alone in a big cold bed all by myself. An' my maw, she brought me her own pillah and she put it under the covers next to me. And she said to pretend it was one o' *them* keepin' me warm through the night and watchin' over me. Pore Maw. She slep' without a pillah for a coupla months there. (*He takes her in his arms and kisses her.*) Now *your* job is to get the *other* side o' the bed warm for me! (*Under the covers,* MARY *runs her hands on* JAY's *side of the bed and warms it. There is the sudden sharp ring of the TELEPHONE downstairs. All sound, all movement stops for a moment. The RING is repeated.* MARY *sits up in bed and* JAY *goes out grumbling.*) Now who could that be this time o' night? (*He goes down to the kitchen and answers the telephone.*) Hello—? Yeah, Central, this is Jay Follet—put 'im through. Hello, Ralph? What's the trouble? Ralph? Sure I can hear you, what's the matter? Are you cryin', Ralph? (*Impatiently.*) Paw? Listen, Ralph, I 'preciate your calling and you're *not* putting me out—now tell me about Paw. (*He listens.*) I should come up, huh? (*Suddenly angry.*) Hold on, Ralph, you hold on there! I'm glad I'm not where I could hit you—! If Paw's that bad you know damn well I'm comin', so don't give me none o' that! Will you stop *cryin'*! Now listen to me, Ralph, I want you to get it straight I'm not tryin' to jump on you, but sometimes you're likely to exaggerate and—no, I don't think you're alyin' to me—and no, I don't think you're drunk! I just want you to think for a minute! *Just how sick is he really,* Ralph? (*In a fury.*) *Think,* God-damn it! (MARY *has followed him downstairs, turned on the kitchen LIGHT, lighted the stove, put a few fresh grounds into the coffee pot and placed it on the flame. She is now sitting in the chair left of the table, listening.*) Listen, Ralph, I know you wouldn'ta phoned if you didn't think it was serious.

MARY. (*Whispering.*) Is Sally there?

JAY. Is Sally out to the farm? And 'course Maw's there.

MARY. Doctor?

JAY. And the doctor? What's he say?— From the way you tell me that, I suspect the doctor said a *good* chance. (*Now anxious to hang up.*) Look here, Ralph, I'm talkin' too much. I'm startin' right on up. I ought to be there by—what time is it now?

MARY. (*Looking at clock.*) It's eleven-thirty.

JAY. It's eleven-thirty, Ralph. I ought to be there by two, two-thirty. Well, I'm afraid that's the best my ole Tin Lizzy can make it, Ralph. You tell Maw I'm comin' right on up quick's I can.

MARY. Is he conscious?

JAY. Is he conscious? Well, if he gets conscious, just let him know I'm comin'! That's all right, Ralph. Don't mention it— Mary understands— Good-bye, Ralph. That's all right— Thanks for calling. *Good-bye, Ralph!* (*He hangs up.*) My God, talkin' to him's like tryin' to put socks on an octopus.

MARY. Is it very grave?

JAY. Lord knows. I can't be sure of anything with Ralph, but I can't afford to take the risk.

MARY. (*To table with cup and saucer.*) Of course not.

JAY. What're *you* up to?

MARY. I'm fixing you something to eat.

JAY. Aw, honey, I'll get a bite on the way if I want to.

MARY. In one of those all-night lunchrooms? Sakes alive!

JAY. It'll be quicker, honest it will. (*He goes upstairs.*)

MARY. I don't want your mother to think I don't feed you.

(*She checks the coffee, runs into the living room, selects a pipe from the rack on the piano, picks up* JAY's *tobacco pouch and returns to the kitchen, putting them on the table by the cup and saucer. She returns to the stove to tend the coffee. During this,* JAY *has been putting on his vest and coat in their bedroom. He is about to go out of the room when he sees the rumpled bed. He smooths out the covers, pulling them high to keep in the warmth. Then, on a sudden thought, he puts his pillow well down under the covers where he would normally sleep. He leaves the room, looks in briefly on Rufus, then goes*

*down into the living room. He selects a pipe,
searches vainly for his tobacco pouch and enters the
kitchen.)*

JAY. Have you seen my tobacco—aw, you had it all
ready for me.

MARY. I had to guess which pipe you wanted to take.

JAY. (*Picking up her choice, slipping his own into his
pocket.*) Just the one I was looking for.

MARY. (*Pleased.*) It's the one I gave you. (*Pulling
back a chair at the table.*) At least you have time for a
cup of coffee. (*As he hesitates.*) It's the way you like it.
(*He grins and sits. She pours the coffee.*) The pot's
choked *full* of old grounds, and I added some new.

JAY. (*Sipping.*) Now that's *coffee*.

MARY. I'd as soon watch you drink sulfuric acid.

JAY. The outing today musta been too much for him.
Paw just sits there so quiet any more we don't always
know what's going on underneath. He got home and just
collapsed.

MARY. Isn't it funny, Jay? This afternoon he was
saying we'd be losing your great-grandmother soon. And
now it turns out your father's the one in danger.

JAY. I guess we never know who's in danger. (*She fills
his cup again.*) You got a birthday coming up. What
would you like to do?

MARY. Why, Jay. Why—you nice thing. Why—

JAY. You think it over. Whatever you'd like best.
Within reason, of course. I'll see we manage it. (*Then
as they* BOTH *remember.*) That is, of course, if everything goes the way we hope it will, up home. (*He goes
into living room where he scrapes out his pipe. She
follows him.*)

MARY. It's time, isn't it? You're almost looking forward to it, aren't you, Jay? The all-night lunchroom.
Driving through the night when everybody else is asleep,
going fast.

JAY. I just know I have to go, Mary. So I'm anxious
to get started.

MARY. (*Giving him a hug.*) Don't drive too fast.

JAY. (*Pointing to the ashtray.*) Scrapelings for him to
find in the morning. For his collection.

MARY. I wonder if we should wake him up. I'm afraid he's going to be disappointed you didn't tell him good-bye.

JAY. I've looked in on him. Tell you what. Tell him, don't promise him or anything, of course, but tell him I'm practically sure to be back before he's asleep tomorrow night. Tell him I'll do my best.

MARY. All right, Jay. Give my love to your mother. Tell her they're both in my thoughts and wishes constantly. And your father, of course, if he's—well enough to talk. (*By now they are at the back door.*)

JAY. Don't you come any further.

MARY. (*Feeling a chill.*) It was so warm this afternoon. (*He kisses her.*) I wish I could go with you, Jay. In whatever happens.

JAY. Why'd you add that?

MARY. It's the way I feel.

JAY. (*He kisses her again.*) I'll let you know quick's I can, if it's serious. (*He goes across the yard rapidly. She stands in the door. He stops, halfway.*) Hey, how's your money?

MARY. (*Thinking quickly.*) All right, thank you.

JAY. Tell *him* I'll even try to make it for supper!

MARY. All right, dear.

JAY. Good night.

MARY. Good night.

JAY. (*He goes to the edge of the stage and turns back once more. In a loud whisper.*) I keep forgettin' to tell you! I want this next one to be a girl!

(*He goes. She stands waiting in the door, but is chilled again and goes inside, turns off stove and kitchen LIGHT, goes upstairs. She sees the lump on the bed, pulls back the covers wonderingly, then she smiles.*)

MARY. The dear. Why, the dear. (*She gets into bed and hugs the pillow as:*)

THE CURTAIN FALLS

ACT TWO

AT RISE: CATHERINE *is sitting in chair Left of kitchen table.* MARY *is measuring a slipcover which she is making for the living room davenport.*

CATHERINE. Father Jackson and I have had the loveliest afternoon planning aid to war-stricken Europe. And since we were all to come here for supper, I saw no reason for going home, only to come out again. So I thought I'd stop by early, Mary dear, and we could have a nice quiet chat.

MARY. Lovely, Mama.

CATHERINE. (*Lifting her ear trumpet.*) Beg pardon?

MARY. (*Into trumpet.*) We can have a nice quiet chat!

CATHERINE. Lovely. Of course when your papa finds out I've been with Father Jackson, there's no telling what he'll say. (*Dropping her ear trumpet firmly to her lap.*) Well, I simply shan't listen.

MARY. Mama! (*The TELEPHONE rings and MARY starts for the kitchen.*)

CATHERINE. Bathroom?

MARY. Telephone!! (*She answers.*) Hello? Yes, Central, go ahead— Jay? Jay darling, I've been so anxious all day. How's your father? Oh dear, then you went all that way for nothing. Now there's no sense in getting angry about it, darling, you know Ralph—just be thankful your father's all right. (RUFUS *runs down the stairs and starts to tiptoe out.*) Rufus, come say hello to Grandma Lynch. (*He puts out his hand to* CATHERINE *who hugs him.*) Where's your hat?

RUFUS. I forgot.

MARY. Well, *get* it, darling. (RUFUS *goes into the living room where he pulls his hat out from under his jacket where he has hidden it.*) What's that, dear? Oh, then you'll definitely be here for supper—the family's coming up—

36

CATHERINE. (*Overlapping.*) Give Jay my love.

MARY. Yes, Mama's here already and she sends her love. The others are coming up later and Andrew has a present for me that they're all being very mysterious about, so do try to make it, Jay. Well, don't hurry, not if it means driving fast, because I can hold supper—I'd rather hold it than have you race—all right, darling, we'll see you very soon then—thank you for calling—good-bye. (*She hangs up.*) Excuse me!! (*She goes into the living room.*) Rufus, what are you doing under there—? You're supposed to be at the street car stop.

RUFUS. (*Climbing out from under the piano bench where he has been searching for something.*) I was looking for the surprise.

MARY. The surprise?

RUFUS. Daddy said it was in here some place.

MARY. Oh Rufus, oh darling—!

RUFUS. He said so, didn't he?

MARY. (*Adjusting his hat.*) Now don't ask questions, darling, you *can't* keep Aunt Hannah waiting. That was Daddy on the telephone and Grampa Follet's going to be all right! Isn't that wonderful? And Daddy said he'd be home in time for supper—think of that, Rufus! You'll see him before you go to bed! (*Stepping back to survey his appearance.*) Now—what are you going to say to Aunt Hannah?

RUFUS. (*As if reciting a piece in school.*) I am glad to go shopping with you—

MARY. *So* glad.

RUFUS. I am so glad to go shopping with you, Aunt Hannah, and thank you for—

MARY. Thank you *very much.*

RUFUS. And thank you very much for thinking of me.

MARY. Now say it all together.

RUFUS. I-am-so-glad-to-go-shopping-with-you-Aunt-Hannah-and-thank-you-very-much-for-thinking-of me!

MARY. (*Laughs and kisses him.*) And be sure to help with her parcels.

CATHERINE. You always dress him so well, Mary dear.

(*They go into the back part of the house. Alone,* RUFUS

takes off his hat and stuffs it contemptuously under his jacket. The LIGHTS dim in the house.)

RUFUS. (*Placing one foot ahead of the other, balances, and sings softly.*)
"I'm a little busy bee, busy bee, busy bee,
I'm a little busy bee, singing in the clover!"

(*The older* BOYS *return, pushing a home-made cart with an elaborate, mast-like steering rod.*)

FIRST BOY. Hey busy bee—
SECOND BOY. Bzz-bzz-bzz!
FIRST BOY. What's your name?
RUFUS. You know.
FIRST BOY. No I don't. Tell me.
SECOND BOY. Bzzzzzzzzzzzz—!
RUFUS. I told you yesterday.
FIRST BOY. No honest! I don't know your name!
THIRD BOY. He wouldn't ast you if he knowed it already, would he?
RUFUS. You're just trying to tease me.
SECOND BOY. I don't think he's got a name at all! He's a no-name nothin'!
THIRD BOY. No-name nothin'!
FIRST BOY. Leave 'im alone! Stop pickin' on 'im! What d'you mean, pickin' on a little kid like that! Pick on someone your own size!
THIRD BOY. (*The picture of innocence.*) I didn't mean nothin'!
FIRST BOY. (*To* RUFUS.) Don't pay no 'tention to *them!* (RUFUS *looks longingly at the cart.*) Yeah, get on up. (RUFUS *climbs on eagerly, tests the steering rod, then puts out his hand gratefully.*) What you puttin' your hand out for?
RUFUS. So you can shake it. (*The* BOYS *giggle, but the* FIRST BOY *shushes them up.*)
FIRST BOY. I'll tell you what—I'll shake it if you'll tell me your name.
RUFUS. (*Suddenly bold.*) I'll tell you my name if you'll answer a question!

38

FIRST BOY. What question?

RUFUS. You've got to promise to answer it first.

FIRST BOY. Cross my heart and body! Now what's your name?

RUFUS. (*He looks from one to the other. They wait, respectful and interested.*) It's Rufus.

(*The minute it is out of his mouth, the* BOYS *scream and jeer as loudly as they can:*)

THE BOYS. Nigger name! Nigger name! Nigger name!

RUFUS. It is not either! I got it from my Great-Grampa Lynch!

THIRD BOY. Then your grampa's a nigger too!

(*They run through all their chants, adding "Rufus' Grampa's a nigger!"*)

RUFUS. It's my *great*-grampa and he is *not!*

THE BOYS. He's a ning-ger! He's a ning-ger!

(HANNAH LYNCH *is suddenly in their midst.*)

HANNAH. (*Peering near-sightedly.*) Now what's all this!

(*The* BOYS, *at once subdued, murmur "Afternoon, Ma'am!" And "We gotta go!" and "Yeah, it's time!" Backing away, and suddenly running off.*)

RUFUS. (*Yelling after them.*) You didn't answer my question—!

HANNAH. (*Observing his distraught state.*) Never mind, Rufus, see what I've brought you. (*She gives him a small bag. He looks inside. She waits for him to be pleased. But he turns to look after the departed boys.*) Well—?

RUFUS. They didn't play fair.

HANNAH. There are chocolate drops in there, Rufus, and speckled pennies and I don't know what all. I was **almost** *late* picking them out.

RUFUS. (*Clutching the bag.*) Thank you, Aunt Hannah.

HANNAH. Don't you think it would be polite to offer me one?

RUFUS. Will you have a piece of my candy, Aunt Hannah?

HANNAH. Why, thank you, Rufus, for thinking of me. I'd like a chocolate drop, if you'll pick it out for me. My eyes, you know. (*He digs for the candy. She looks up the street.*) How many street cars have we missed?

RUFUS. I don't know.

HANNAH. What was the question you wanted to ask those boys? Perhaps I can help you.

RUFUS. Mama says we've got a surprise coming to our house.

HANNAH. Why were you going to ask those boys about it?

RUFUS. Because Daddy said if Mama didn't tell me about it, I'd find out from the older boys in the street.

HANNAH. And she didn't tell you?

RUFUS. She and Daddy had a fight about it, and now Mama won't let me ask questions at all.

HANNAH. I see. (*She considers this for a moment.*) Rufus, aren't you going to eat your candy?

RUFUS. The teacher says we should send things to the Belgian orphans.

HANNAH. Well, that's very generous of you, but I bought the candy for *you,* in case you grow tired of traipsing from store to store, for we have a great deal of shopping to do this afternoon. A scarf for your mother's birthday—you mustn't tell her!—and something called A Grammar of Ornament for your Uncle Andrew, and bunion pads for me, and hooks and eyes—

RUFUS. (*Eagerly.*) Can I watch you pare your bunions?

HANNAH. We'll see. But for the time being, I'm sure the Belgian orphans wouldn't mind if you had one piece of their candy.

RUFUS. Would *you* like another piece of my candy, Aunt Hannah?

HANNAH. Thank you, Rufus, a speckled penny this time I think. (*He gives her one.*)

RUFUS. What do those boys know about a surprise that's coming to our house, Aunt Hannah? Did Daddy tell them?

HANNAH. Of course not. They don't know a thing.

RUFUS. Daddy said they did.

HANNAH. He didn't mean they *knew* exactly, he just meant they— (*She stops, at a loss, and takes her glasses off, holding them up to the light.*) Rufus, I'm sure your mother saw to it that you had a clean handkerchief before you came out of the house.

RUFUS. (*Excitedly.*) Can I clean your glasses, Aunt Hannah?

HANNAH. If you'll promise to be *very* careful.

RUFUS. I promise!

HANNAH. (*Handing him the glasses.*) I'll hold the candy for you. (*He gives her the bag of candy and she munches absent-mindedly during the following.*) Rufus, *I* know about the surprise.

RUFUS. (*Astonished.*) You *do?*

HANNAH. Oh, yes. And I could tell you about it. But there are certain things that should only be told by certain people. For instance, your teacher should be the one to tell you about arithmetic, because she knows about it. And a Priest, or a Minister, should be the one to tell you about God because he's a *man* of God. And your Mama and daddy are the only ones to tell you about this particular surprise. Oh, there are others who'd be *willing* to tell you about it, if you ask them. But you mustn't ask them.

RUFUS. Why not, Aunt Hannah?

HANNAH. Because they wouldn't tell it right.

RUFUS. Wouldn't *you* tell it right?

HANNAH. (*After a moment.*) Breathe on the lenses, child. That's right. (*She holds out her hand and he gives her the glasses.*) You wait for your mama to explain. You'll be glad later on. (*Her glasses are on now and she leans close to peer at him.*) *There* you are! (*He laughs, delighted.*) What's that bunchy place under your jacket?

RUFUS. (*Guilty.*) My hat.

HANNAH. Well, let's put it on. (*She pulls out and smooths the rumpled hat, examining it distastefully.*) Where *does* your mother buy your clothes? (*She looks at the label inside his jacket collar.*) Millers? (*He nods. She plunks the hat on his head.*) Hmp. *Women's clothes* cut to fit little boys. After we've done our shopping on Gay Street, I think we'll go around to Market Street.

RUFUS. (*Intrigued.*) Mama won't *go* on Market *Street*.

HANNAH. We're going into Harbison's there. (*With satisfaction.*) I hear they're *very* sporty. And I'm going to buy you a cap. (*He is speechless.*) Or is there something else you'd rather have?

RUFUS. (*Passionately.*) Oh no—no!

HANNAH. (*Pleased.*) We'll see what we can do about it. (*Taking her change purse from her bag.*) Now, Rufus, when a gentleman takes a lady out for an afternoon of shopping, *he's* the one to pay for everything. So I'm going to let you carry my money. First of all, you'll need street car fares— (*She puts two coins into the palm of his hand.*) Five cents for you and five cents for me. Or would you rather walk? Then you can keep the street car fares for yourself.

RUFUS. (*In seventh heaven. He begins to tug her off stage.*) Oh-Aunt-Hannah-I'm-so-glad-to-go-shopping-with-you-and-thank you-very-much-for-thinking-of me.

HANNAH. Your mother told you to say that, didn't she?

RUFUS. I forgot.

HANNAH. (*As they start off.*) I know direct quotation when I hear it.

(*The LIGHTS dim. In the dark, MARY sings "Go tell Aunt Rhodie" as she sits by Rufus' bed. The LIGHTS come up on CATHERINE at the piano, running her fingers over the keys but playing no music. JOEL comes in and watches her, ANDREW comes into the yard by the swing and spreads a quilt on the ground. During the following, HANNAH enters the kitchen from the unseen dining room and finishes straightening up around the sink.*)

CATHERINE. I wish you wouldn't stand there, Joel. I can't do my best when I'm being watched.

JOEL. What the devil do you think you're playing?

CATHERINE. The Burning of Rome.

JOEL. Well, let's hear it, then.

CATHERINE. Rufus is asleep! (*She turns a page and goes on "Playing."*)

JOEL. Good God! (*He crosses out to the yard and Down Right.*)

ANDREW. (*Resting against glider.*) You know, Papa, we've got to face the possibility, you and I, that Jay is drunk somewhere and be ready for it!

JOEL. Rot!

ANDREW. Mary's thinking it though—ever since supper—and she's worried, I can tell, Papa—she's got what Jay calls that pursed-up look. Shall I go look for him?

JOEL. Where would you look?

ANDREW. He used to like those places down off Market Square. It's lively down there at night, Papa, with the farmers rolling into town and the smell of salt and leather and fresh vegetables and whiskey!

JOEL. If that's where he is, let the man come home on his own. It will be hard enough for him when he gets here. You might as well learn, Andrew, it's the way of our women to try to break their men with piety.

ANDREW. Or is it the way of our men, Papa, to try to break their women with impiety? (JOEL *snorts.*) I'm just asking. I've never been able to decide who I am, your son or Mama's.

JOEL. Not everyone has such a wide choice.

(MARY *has stopped singing, gone down the stairs and now passes through the kitchen.*)

MARY. Rufus is finally asleep. He was terribly disappointed that Jay hadn't come home.

HANNAH. He'll be along soon.

MARY. (*She crosses out to yard and sits beside* JOEL *on the swing.*) Do you think I've been deserted, Papa? Do you think my husband's gone away, never to return? Will you take care of me again, Papa, if I'm deserted?

43

Will you let me come home again and sit on your lap and cry for my lost love?

JOEL. No, daughter.

MARY. Why not, Papa?

JOEL. Because you'll never be deserted.

MARY. You always defend Jay, don't you, Papa?

JOEL. I always thought highly of him. From the first.

MARY. You'd praise Jay to the skies on the one hand, and on the other, why practically in the same breath, you'd be telling me one reason after another why it would be plain foolhardy to marry him.

JOEL. Isn't it possible that I meant both things?

MARY. I don't see how.

JOEL. You learned how yourself, Mary.

MARY. Is that what I've learned?

JOEL. I've taken Jay into the office. That shows confidence.

MARY. And he's teaching himself law! Your confidence is justified!

JOEL. (*Laughing.*) That's what I wanted. To hear you defend him!

MARY. Me defend him—? Why, Papa, why— I couldn't ever defend Jay enough! Oh Papa, in these past few months we've come to a—a kind of harmoniousness that is so beautiful I've no business talking about it. It's only the gulfs between us. If I could fill them in, it would all be perfect. I want life to be perfect, Papa. (*Looking off.*) Why doesn't he come home? (*Turning back to them.*) Andrew, I'm ready to see that present now!

ANDREW. (*Going into the living room as the others follow.*) I should make you wait for your birthday, Mary, it was meant to be a birthday present.

MARY. What is it, a new picture you've done?

JOEL. I think you'll like it, Mary.

HANNAH. Yes, Mary!

MARY. Oh, you've all seen it! (*Ad-libs from* OTHERS.)

ANDREW. Mama, will you give us a nice fanfare for the unveiling?

JOEL. She didn't hear you, Andrew.

MARY. Mama, Andrew wonders if you could play a

44

fanfare! (CATHERINE *does so.* ANDREW *reveals the picture.*) Oh, Andrew. It's Jay.

ANDREW. Do you like it?

MARY. It *is* Jay!

HANNAH. I think Andrew caught a very good likeness.

JOEL. Especially around the mouth and chin.

MARY. Yes, right in through there, especially.

ANDREW. The eyes were the hardest. They always are unless the subject sits for you, and I didn't want Jay to do that because then you'd both have known. I've been making sketches for months.

MARY. He wouldn't have done it anyhow. Imagine Jay sitting still for an artist. (CATHERINE *nods yes.*)

HANNAH. The picture has great dignity.

JOEL. So has Jay.

MARY. (*Hugging* ANDREW.) Oh Andrew, I just love it! Thank you!

RUFUS. (*He runs down the stairs calling.*) Daddy! Daddy!

MARY. Oh, dear!

HANNAH. I guess we *were* making a racket.

(RUFUS *runs into the room, wearing his night shirt and a thunderous fleecy check cap in jade green, canary yellow, black and white, which sticks out inches to either side above his ears and has a great scoop of a visor beneath which his face is all but lost.*)

CATHERINE. There's little Rufus!

RUFUS. Did Daddy come home yet?

MARY. No, dear, what made you think so?

RUFUS. I woke up. I wanted to show him my cap!

MARY. Rufus, I told you not to wear that cap to bed! (*Exasperated.*) Aunt Hannah! I'll never *forgive* you. (HANNAH *smiles rather secretly and shrugs.*)

CATHERINE. Rufus, come give Grandma a good hug! (RUFUS *goes to her and hugs her. She vigorously slaps his back.*) Mmm-mm. Nice little boy! (*Over his shoulder to* MARY, *gently reproving.*) Mary dear, do you think he ought to wear his cap to *bed?* (*They* ALL *laugh.*)

45

(The TELEPHONE rings.)

MARY. Maybe that's Jay. *(She goes quickly to the kitchen.)*

CATHERINE. *(Discreetly to HANNAH.)* Bathroom?

RUFUS. *(Loudly.)* Telephone! *(CATHERINE nods and smiles.)*

MARY. *(At telephone.)* Hello—?

CATHERINE. *(Taking RUFUS' hand.)* Come along, Rufus, let *Grandma* put you to bed *this* time! *(She takes him upstairs.)*

MARY. *(Loudly.)* Hello! Will you please talk a little louder! I can't hear—I said I can't hear you!

JOEL. It's long distance all right.

HANNAH. Oh dear, his father's worse.

ANDREW. At least we know where he is!

(They try not to listen, focusing on the portrait, but gradually they are caught by what they can hear.)

MARY. Yes that's better, thank you. Yes, this is she, what is it? *(A long silence.)* Yes—I heard you. *(She stares dumbly at the telephone, then rallies.)* Yes, there's my brother. Where should he come to? *(Closing her eyes, concentrating, memorizing.)* Brannick's—left of the Pike —Bell's Bridge. Do you have a doctor? A *doctor,* do you have one? All right then—my brother will come out just as fast as he can. Thank you—very much for calling. Good night. *(She hangs up and stands for a moment, her hand still on the telephone. Then she slowly returns to the* OTHERS.*)* Andrew, there's been an—that was a man from Powell's station, about twelve miles out towards LaFollette, and he says—he says Jay has met with a very serious accident. He wants—he said they want some man of his family to come out just as soon as possible and— help bring him in, I guess.

ANDREW. Shall I get Dr. Dekalb?

MARY. He says no. Just you.

ANDREW. I guess there's a doctor already there.

MARY. I guess so.

ANDREW. Where do I go?

46

MARY. Powell's Station, out on the Pike toward—

ANDREW. I know, but exactly where? Didn't he say?

MARY. Brannick's Blacksmith Shop. B-r-a-n-n-i-c-k. He said they'll keep the lights on and you can't miss it. It's just to the left of the Pike, just this side of Bell's Bridge.

ANDREW. I won't be any longer than I have to.

MARY. Bless you. I'll—we'll get everything ready here in case—you know—he's well enough to be brought home.

ANDREW. Good. I'll phone the minute I know anything. Anything.

MARY. Bless you, dear. (ANDREW *goes.*)

JOEL. Where is he hurt?

MARY. He didn't say.

JOEL. Well, didn't you ask—?

HANNAH. Joel.

JOEL. No matter.

MARY. Where's Mama?

JOEL. Upstairs with Rufus.

MARY. Keep her up there, will you, Papa—? Just a few minutes till I— Make sure Rufus is asleep, be sure he's asleep, then tell her what's happened. And talk as softly as you can and still have her know what you're saying.

JOEL. Would you like us to go home, Mary?

MARY. No!

JOEL. We'll keep out of the way—

MARY. It's not that—it's just that with Mama it's so very hard to talk.

HANNAH. For heaven's sake, Joel, go along. (*He goes.*)

MARY. What time is it, Aunt Hannah?

HANNAH. About ten-twenty-five.

MARY. Let's see, Andrew drives pretty fast, though not so fast as Jay, but he'll be driving better than usual tonight, and it's just over twelve miles. That would be— supposing he goes thirty miles an hour, that's twelve miles—let's see, six times four is twenty-four, six times five's thirty, twice twelve is twenty-four—sakes alive, I was always dreadful at figures.

HANNAH. It's only 12 miles. We should hear very soon.

47

MARY. (*Abruptly.*) Let's have some tea.

HANNAH. Why not let me— (*She stops.*)

MARY. (*Blankly.*) What?

HANNAH. Just let me know if there's anything I can help with.

MARY. Not a thing, thank you. (*She goes into the kitchen, and during the following lights the stove, puts the kettle on to boil, takes down the box of tea, finds the strainer, the cups and saucers. HANNAH watches, her hands folded.*) We'll make up the downstairs bedroom. Remember he stayed there when his poor back was sprained. It's better than upstairs, near the kitchen and the bathroom and no stairs to climb. He's always saying we must get the bathroom upstairs but we never do. And of course, if need be, that is if he needs a nurse, we can put her in the dining room and eat in here, or even set up a cot right in the room with him and put up a screen. Or if she minds that, why she can just sleep on the living room davenport and keep the door open in between. Don't you think so?

HANNAH. Certainly.

MARY. Of course it's very possible he'll have to be taken straight to a hospital. The man did say it was serious, after all. Sugar and milk— (*She gets them.*)— or lemon. I don't know if I have any lemons, Aunt Hannah—

HANNAH. Milk is fine for me.

MARY. Me too. Would you like some Zuzus? (*She gets them from the cupboard.*) Or bread and butter, or toast? I could toast some.

HANNAH. Just tea will do.

MARY. Well, here are the Zuzus. (*She puts them on the table.*)

HANNAH. Thank you.

MARY. Goodness sakes, the watched *pot!* (*She stands by the stove, motionless.*)

HANNAH. I hope you didn't really mind my giving Rufus that cap, Mary.

MARY. (*Vaguely.*) Heavens no, you were good to do it.

HANNAH. I'm sure if you had realized how much he wanted one, you'd have given it to him yourself long ago.

MARY. (*Forcing concentration.*) Of course. Oh, yes. But *Harbisons*, isn't that where you got it? I hear it's so tough, how did you ever dare go *in?*

HANNAH. Fortunately, I'm so blind I couldn't see what might hurt me. I just sailed up to the nearest man and said, "Where do I go, please, to find a cap for my nephew?" And he said, "I'm no clerk, Ma'am, I'm a customer myself." And I said, "Then why aren't you wearing a hat?" He had no answer to *that*, of course, so—

MARY. Why didn't he tell me!

HANNAH. Who?

MARY. That man on the telephone? Why didn't I ask! I didn't even ask! *How* serious! *Where* is he hurt! Papa noticed it!

HANNAH. You couldn't think.

MARY. Is he living or dead! (*She has said it.*)

HANNAH. That we simply have to wait and find out.

MARY. Of course we have to wait! That's what's so unbearable!

HANNAH. Try if you can to find a mercy in it.

MARY. A *mercy*—?

HANNAH. A little time to prepare ourselves.

MARY. I'm sorry, Aunt Hannah, you're quite right. (*She sits in chair Right of table.*)

CATHERINE. (*Crossing to head of stairs, followed by* JOEL.) I'm going down to see if there isn't something I can do for poor dear Mary. (JOEL *stops her.*) But it's my place to, isn't it, Joel? (*She continues downstairs.*)

MARY. I don't know's I really want any tea but I think it's a good idea to drink something warm while we're waiting, don't you?

HANNAH. (*Crosses up for tea kettle and strainer.*) I'd like some.

CATHERINE. I've decided there is no cause for alarm, Mary dear. Jay is perfectly all right, I'm sure. And Andrew was simply too overjoyed with relief to bother to phone and is bringing Jay straight home instead for a wonderful surprise. That would be like Andrew. And like Jay to go along with the surprise and enjoy it, just laugh at how scared we've been. Of course, we shall have

49

to scold them both. (MARY *rises to cupboard.* CATHERINE *crosses to living room, sits on sofa Left of* JOEL.) Joel, what Andrew's doing is to come in with Jay's poor body to the undertaker's. Roberts, probably. Although they do say that new man over on Euclid Avenue is very good. But our family has always used Roberts.

MARY. Did Rufus pick out the cap all by himself?

HANNAH. You don't think I chose that monstrosity, do you? (*She laughs.*) At first he picked a very genteel little serge, but I smelled the hypocrisy behind it, and forgive an old woman, Mary, but I said, "Do you really like that one or do you just think it will please your mother?" Then he revealed his true taste. But I was switched if I was going to boss him.

MARY. (*Who has not listened.*) Either he's badly hurt but he'll live. Or he is so terribly hurt that he will die from it, maybe after a long, terrible, struggle, maybe breathing his last at this very minute and wondering where I am, why I'm not there. Or he was already gone when the man called. Of course it's just what we have no earthly business guessing about. And I'm not going to say he's dead until I know for sure that he is.

HANNAH. Certainly not.

MARY. But I'm all but certain that he is, all the same. (*After a moment.*) Oh I do beseech my God that it be not so! (*Turning to* HANNAH, *lost, scared.*) Aunt Hannah, can we kneel down for a moment? (HANNAH *does not respond.*) Aunt *Hannah*—?

HANNAH. (*Sighing.*) No, Mary.

MARY. (*Bewildered.*) Why not—?

HANNAH. It's too easy. As you say, it's one thing or the other. But no matter what it is, there's not one thing in this world or the next that we can do or hope or guess at or wish or pray that can change it one iota. Because whatever it is, *is*. That's all. And all there is now is to be ready for it, strong enough for it, whatever it may be. That's all that matters because it's all that's possible.

MARY. I'm *trying* to be ready—!

HANNAH. Your beliefs have never been truly tested. God has come easily to you. He's going to come harder

50

now. But if you wait until you can't go on without Him, you'll find Him. When you *have* to pray, we'll pray.

MARY. Goodness sakes, why don't I get his room ready? (*Crosses into living room, then into back part of the house.*)

HANNAH. It's your turn now.

CATHERINE. What time is it, Joel?

JOEL. Twelve-forty-five. A quarter of one!

CATHERINE. Andrew's had time to get there and back, hasn't he, Joel?

JOEL. Twice!

CATHERINE. Don't shout at me, Joel. Just speak distinctly and I can hear you. (*She crosses Down Left to below the piano and gets her ear trumpet.*) Just think, Joel, it will be a posthumous baby.

JOEL. Good—God, woman.

CATHERINE. We haven't had a posthumous birth in the family since—your cousin Hetty was posthumous, wasn't she? Of course, your Uncle Henry was killed in the War Between the States.

MARY. (*Who has joined HANNAH in the kitchen, begins to pray.*) Our Father, Who art in Heaven— (*As they say the prayer, ANDREW enters and rushes to HANNAH's arms. He holds her so close that she gasps.*)

ANDREW. Mary!

MARY. He's dead, Andrew, isn't he? He was dead when you got there.

ANDREW. (*He has withdrawn to the swing.*) He was instantly killed!

MARY. (*She starts to go limp.*) Papa—! Mama—!

(*He supports her as best he can into the living room where the OTHERS take her from him and seat her on the davenport.*)

CATHERINE. There there there, Mary, dear, there there!

HANNAH. (*She goes to get water and then smelling salts.*) Sit down, Mary—!

JOEL. It's hell, Mary, just plain hell!

ANDREW. (*Hysterically.*) Instantly, Papa! Instantly! (*Snapping his fingers again and again.*) Instantly! Quick

51

as that! Quick as that! He was at this blacksmith's shop and they made me look at him! Instantly! This reeking horseblanket and they made me look! I'd never seen a dead man before and it was Jay! Instantly! The flat of the hand! The flat of the hand of death, the flat of the hand—! (*He is now slapping the seat of a kitchen chair.*)

JOEL. For God's sake, Andrew, think of your sister!

MARY. What happened, Andrew?

HANNAH. Give yourself a minute, Mary, just a minute—

CATHERINE. (*Waving the smelling salts past* MARY'S *nose.*) This will clear your head—

MARY. (*Brushing the salts aside.*) I don't want it, Mama, I want to hear what happened! Andrew?

ANDREW. (*As if suddenly realizing.*) I have to tell you—?

JOEL. Tell her!

ANDREW. I can't, I can't be the one—!

JOEL. What *happened?*

ANDREW. I don't even know how to begin—!

JOEL. Just begin!

ANDREW. Where?

JOEL. Anywhere.

ANDREW. Well—he was alone, for one thing—

MARY. Of course he was alone, I *know* that.

ANDREW. I just meant—there was no one else in the accident, or other automobiles—

MARY. I want to hear about *Jay!*

ANDREW. I'm *trying* to tell you—!

JOEL. *What caused the accident?*

ANDREW. (*Shouting.*) A cotter pin!

MARY. What's a cotter pin?

ANDREW. You wouldn't understand, Mary, you don't know about automobiles—

MARY. Papa, make him tell me!

ANDREW. All *right,* it's just something that holds the steering mechanism together like this— (*Holds up his knuckles.*) There'd be a hole through the knuckles and that's where the cotter pin goes like a hairpin and you open the ends flat and spread them—

MARY. I *understand!*

ANDREW. *The cotter pin fell out.*

MARY. What happened then?

ANDREW. Nobody was there, we can't say. He just lost control of the auto!

MARY. Who found him?

ANDREW. The man who telephoned you.

MARY. Who was he?

ANDREW. I don't know his name.

MARY. I wish you did.

ANDREW. He was driving in toward town about nine o'clock and he heard Jay coming up from behind terrifically fast— All of a sudden he said he heard a terrifying noise and then dead silence. He turned around and drove back—

MARY. Where was this?

ANDREW. Just the other side of Bell's Bridge—

MARY. Where you come down that sort of angle?

ANDREW. That's the place. He'd been thrown absolutely clear of the auto as it ran off the road. And the car had gone up an eight-foot embankment, then tumbled back, bottom-side up, right next to him, without even grazing him. They think when this cotter pin fell out, he must have been thrown forward very hard, so he struck his chin one sharp blow against the steering wheel, and that must have killed him—

MARY. (*Putting her hand to his mouth.*) Killed— (*Then, after a long moment.*) I'll never see him again. Never. Never, never, never, never. (*She moves into the living room. The* OTHERS *watch helplessly, unable to comfort or even touch her, for when they try, she tears herself away from them, then she falls to her knees in front of* JAY'S *portrait in the armchair. She is completely dissolved, moaning and crying.* CATHERINE *kneels beside her and puts her arms around her.*)

CATHERINE. There, there, Mary. We're all here.

MARY. (*Now completely drained.*) Thank heaven for that, Mama. (*Weakly.*) Andrew, I want whiskey.

HANNAH. It'll do her good.

JOEL. Do us all good.

ANDREW. I'll go down home and get some.

MARY. No— (*She points vaguely to the hall closet.*

HANNAH *gets the bottle as* ANDREW *is getting glasses. In his haste, he drops one into the sink and it breaks. They pour some for* MARY, *but she holds up her glass for more. Then she gulps it several times. Eventually:*) Did you—what did he look like—?

ANDREW. His clothes were hardly even rumpled.

MARY. (*Nodding.*) His brown suit.

ANDREW. (*At a loss.*) He was lying on his back.

MARY. His face?

ANDREW. Just a little blue bruise on the lower lip.

MARY. (*Hurt.*) Is that all?

ANDREW. And a cut so small they can sew it up with one stitch.

MARY. Where?

ANDREW. The exact point of his chin.

MARY. (*Touching her father's chin.*) Point of the chin, Papa.

ANDREW. The doctor said death was instantaneous. Concussion of the brain. (*She turns away and he stops for a moment. Then she gulps her whiskey and turns back.*) He can't have suffered, Mary, not a fraction of a second. I asked about that very particularly because I knew you'd want to be sure. I saw his face. There wasn't a glimmer of pain in it. Only a kind of surprise. Startled.

MARY. (*Nodding.*) I imagine so.

ANDREW. It was just a chance in a million. Just that one tiny area, at just a certain angle, and just a certain sharpness of impact on the chin. If it had been even half an inch to one side, he'd be alive this minute.

JOEL. Shut up, Andrew.

ANDREW. What'd I say, Papa?

MARY. Have a little mercy! A little mercy!

ANDREW. I'm so sorry, Mary—

HANNAH. Let her cry.

ANDREW. I'm so sorry.

MARY. O God, forgive me! Forgive me! Forgive me! It's just more than I can bear! Just more than I can bear. Forgive me!

ANDREW. Forgive *you!* I say, O God if you exist, God-damn you!

HANNAH. Andrew! (*A silence.*) Mary, listen to me.

54

There's nothing to ask forgiveness for. There's nothing to ask forgiveness for, Mary. Do you hear me, do you hear me, Mary?

MARY. I spoke to Him as if He had no mercy.

HANNAH. Andrew was just—

MARY. To *God*. As if He were trying to rub it in. Torment me! That's what I asked forgiveness for.

CATHERINE. There there, Mary.

HANNAH. Listen, Mary, Our Lord on the Cross, do you remember?

MARY. My God, my God, why hast Thou forsaken me?

HANNAH. Yes. And then did He ask forgiveness?

MARY. He was God. He didn't have to.

HANNAH. He was human too. And He didn't ask it. Nor was it asked of Him to ask it. No more are you. And no more should you. You're wrong. You're terribly mistaken. What was it He said instead? The very next thing?

MARY. Father, into Thy hands— (*She stops.*)

HANNAH. Father, into Thy hands I commend my spirit.

MARY. I commend— (*She stops again, then after a moment, looks up at* HANNAH, *deeply hurt and bewildered.*) You've never had anything *but* God, Aunt Hannah. I had a husband. I was married to a *man*. I won't *have* God in his place. (*She turns away to find herself facing the picture.*) Nor that picture, Andrew. I never saw that face in my life before tonight. Jay's face had eyes and mouth. Put it in the hall closet, Papa.

(JOEL *takes the portrait from the room.*)

CATHERINE. Try not to suffer too much, Mary.

MARY. (*With a sudden, irrational anger.*) That's right, Mama, keep your ear trumpet in your lap! Shut out whatever might be unpleasant! Think of having voices to hear and not listening! (*Stopping, again with that ununderstanding hurt.*) I want more whiskey.

HANNAH. Let me fix you one good hot toddy so you'll sleep.

MARY. I want a *lot* more whiskey!

ANDREW. You'll make yourself drunk, Mary.

MARY. (*Grabbing the bottle angrily.*) Let me!

HANNAH. You've tomorrow to reckon with!

MARY. (*Pouring herself a good drink.*) What's tomorrow? I'm going to get just as drunk as I can. (*She gulps silently.*)

CATHERINE. Mother always said that in times of stress, the best thing to drink was buttermilk.

MARY. (*She laughs.*) Buttermilk!

(ANDREW *laughs, then* HANNAH. JOEL *comes in and joins them in the laughter.*)

JOEL. What are we laughing at? (*They laugh.*)

ANDREW. Buttermilk! (*They laugh.*)

JOEL. What's funny about buttermilk? (*They laugh again.*)

HANNAH. Now, this is terrible. We're not going to laugh any more—we're going to stop it.

MARY. Andrew, stop making me laugh.

HANNAH. Children! Children!

CATHERINE. (*Corking the whiskey bottle, putting it away.*) Well, I never in my life have been so thoroughly shocked and astonished.

(*They are off again on another wave of laughter. There are ad-libs.*)

MARY. (*Suddenly, loudly.*) Listen! (*All the laughing stops and they look to her.*)

ANDREW. What is it?

MARY. Just listen.

JOEL. What's up?

MARY. Quiet, Papa, please. There's something.

ANDREW. I can't hear anything.

HANNAH. (*Who has been watching her closely.*) Mary does.

ANDREW. There is something.

MARY. It's in the kitchen.

ANDREW. I'll go see—

MARY. Wait, Andrew, don't, not yet.

CATHERINE. Has somebody come into the house?

ANDREW. What made you think so, Mama?

CATHERINE. Why, how stupid of me. I thought I heard. Footsteps. I must be getting old and dippy.

ANDREW. Sssh!

MARY. It's Jay.

HANNAH. (*Watching her.*) Of course it is.

JOEL. (*Thundering.*) What—!

MARY. Now he's come into the room with us.

ANDREW. Mary—!

MARY. It's Jay, Andrew, who else would be coming here tonight so terribly worried, so terribly concerned for us, and restless. Feel the restlessness.

ANDREW. You mean you can—

MARY. I mean it simply feels like his presence.

ANDREW. Do you feel anything, Papa?

JOEL. I feel goose bumps, of course. But that's from looking at your faces.

MARY. He's going upstairs.

JOEL. You've got to stop this, Mary.

MARY. Quiet, Papa! He's in Rufus' room.

JOEL. For God's sake, Mary, you're having hallucinations.

HANNAH. Joel, I know that God in a wheelbarrow wouldn't convince you, but Mary *knows* what she is experiencing.

ANDREW. I believe it! I really do!

JOEL. I see you've decided whose son you are.

MARY. Please stop talking about it, please. It just means so much more than we can say. I'd just like to be quiet in the house, by myself. (*She goes upstairs singing "Sugar Babe" softly. The* OTHERS *start to leave.*)

HANNAH. Andrew, when you get home, telephone Jay's people and tell them how it happened.

(MARY *is in Rufus' room. She suddenly calls down to them.*)

MARY. Andrew! (*They stop to look up at her.*) Where is he? Dear God, where is he?

ANDREW. What d'you—?

57

MARY. Where did you take him?

ANDREW. Oh. To Roberts.

MARY. Roberts. Yes. Bless you. (JOEL, CATHERINE *and* ANDREW *go.* MARY *turns into her own room.*) Jay, darling? Dear heart? Are you here? (*She has moved around and stands on the threshold of Rufus' room again.*) JAY—? (*She stops, seeing the little boy sitting up in bed, staring at her. She sinks to the trunk.*) Dear God!

CURTAIN

ACT THREE

At Rise: Rufus *in black is alone in his bedroom. He goes into his mother's room, down the stairs, into the kitchen, then into the living room. No one is around. He takes off his black cap, puts it on the sofa, then from under his jacket takes out his gaudy cap, puts it on and goes out into the street. The* Boys *enter from Down Right on their way to school. The* First Boy *runs past.*

Rufus. My daddy's dead! (*The* Boy *ignores him.*) My daddy's dead!

Second Boy. Huh! Betcha he ain't!

Rufus. Why, he is so.

Second Boy. Where's your satchel at? You're just making up a lie so you can lay outa school.

Rufus. I am not laying out, I'm just staying out, because my daddy's dead!

(*The* Third Boy *has joined them.*)

Third Boy. He can lay out because his daddy got killed. (Rufus *looks at him gratefully. And the* Third Boy *seems to regard him with something like respect.*)

First Boy. How do *you* know?

Third Boy. 'Cause my daddy seen it in the paper. Can't your daddy read?

Rufus. (*Astounded.*) The *news*paper—?

Third Boy. Sure, your daddy got his *name* in the papers. Yours too.

First Boy. (*With growing respect.*) *His* name's in the paper? Rufus's?

Third Boy. Him and his daddy both, right in the paper.

Rufus. He was killed instintly. (*He snaps his fingers.*)

Third Boy. What you get for drivin' a auto when you're drunk, that's what my daddy says.

59

RUFUS. What's drunk?

SECOND BOY. What's *drunk?* Drunk is fulla good ole whiskey. (*He staggers around in circles, weak-kneed, head lolling.*) 'at's what drunk is.

RUFUS. Then he wasn't.

SECOND BOY. How do *you* know?

RUFUS. Because my daddy never walked like that.

THIRD BOY. How'd he get killed if he wasn't drunk?

RUFUS. He had a fatal accident.

SECOND BOY. How'd he *have* a fatal accident if he wasn't drunk?

RUFUS. It was kuhkushon.

SECOND BOY. Hell, you don't even know what you're talkin' about!

FIRST BOY. (*Simultaneously.*) Don't even know how his own daddy got killed! (*They scoff and jeer.* RUFUS *begins to think he has lost his audience.*)

THIRD BOY. My daddy says we gotta feel sorry for Rufus here 'cause he's an orphan.

RUFUS. I am?

THIRD BOY. Sure, like the Belgian kids, on'y worse. 'cause that's *war,* and my daddy says any kid that's made an orphan just 'cause his daddy gets drunk is a *pore kid.*

FIRST BOY. He says his daddy *wasn't* drunk.

SECOND BOY. Yeah.

RUFUS. Maybe he was a little.

FIRST BOY. Izzat so?

RUFUS. I remember now.

THIRD BOY. Sure he was.

SECOND BOY. Good ole whiskey.

THIRD BOY. Pore kid. My daddy says his ole Tin Lizzy run up a eight-foot embankment—

RUFUS. (*Bravely.*) That's all you know about it.

FIRST BOY. (*To* THIRD.) Let *him* tell it.

SECOND BOY. Yeah, *you* tell it, Rufus.

THIRD BOY. Well, come on and tell us then.

RUFUS. Well—it wasn't any old Tin Lizzy he was driving, in the first place, it was a—a Chalmers. And my daddy was going like sixty!

SECOND BOY. 'Cause he was drunk.

RUFUS. (*Nodding.*) Good ole whiskey.

THIRD BOY. Pore kid.

RUFUS. (*Now completely confident.*) And then the auto didn't run up any eight-foot embackemb—what you said—either, it ran up a—a pole.

THIRD BOY. A *pole?*

RUFUS. (*Jumping up on the swing.*) A hundred feet high!

(*Doubts have now set in among the* THREE BOYS.)

SECOND BOY. Aw, what kinduva pole is that?

RUFUS. The *north* pole. (*They stare at him blankly to see if it is an old joke, but he is too excited to notice. He points off.*) Out there! If you squint your eyes you can see it! (*He squints his eyes and peers, searchingly, and the* THREE BOYS *look at one another.* ONE *makes circles with his forefinger at the side of his head,* ANOTHER *silently blubbers his lower lip,* ANOTHER *rolls his eyeballs back so that only the whites are showing.*) Can you see it?

THE THREE BOYS. Oh, yeah! Sure, Rufus! We see it! So that's the North Pole! Hmmm! Always wondered where it was!

RUFUS. And my daddy's auto ran up it and fell right back on top of my daddy like— (*Suddenly he jumps from the swing.*) —whomp! And that joggled his brain loose in his head and it—fell out and the hand of death came down out of the sky and scooped it up. (*Now somewhat out of breath.*) And that's kuhkushon.

FOURTH BOY. (*Running on.*) Hey, I'm waitin' on you.

FIRST BOY. (*Edging off.*) Yeah. Sure, Rufus. Well, we gotta go. (RUFUS *quickly puts out his hand with supreme confidence. The* FIRST BOY *shakes it hurriedly.*) S'long, Rufus.

SECOND BOY. (*Shaking* RUFUS' *hand.*) That's a nice new cap you got, Rufus.

THIRD BOY. (*Shaking hands.*) We'll be seeing yuh, Rufus.

(*They hurry off, looking back over their shoulders*

at him, talking among themselves, one saying "Whomp!" And clapping his hands together, another blubbering his lower lip, another staggering, whether in imitation of a drunk or an imbecile, it is hard to say. RUFUS looks after them, beaming with pride. The BOYS go. RUFUS is alone.)

RUFUS. P-r-o-u-d. *(Scuffing into the living room, making up a song.)* B-r-a-v-e-p-r-o-u-d. *(Gets a pipe, picks up paper, sits in Morris chair.)* "He is sur-sur-vived by his wi-wife, Mary." Mama has her name in the paper. "And a son—Rufus." Me! My daddy's dead. Whomp! He can't ever come home—not tomorrow or the next day or the next day or the next day or the next day or the next day or the next day— *(He is crying. He throws the pipe, newspaper and ashtray aside.)* Whomp! Good ole whiskey! Whomp! Good ole whiskey! Good ole whiskey! Good ole whiskey! Good ole whiskey!

(RUFUS storms about the room, hitting and banging the furniture. Runs into the kitchen and hides under the table. MARY and HANNAH come in.)

MARY. Darling, who have you been talking to—?
RUFUS. My daddy's dead. It says so in the newspaper.
MARY. *(Holding him.)* Oh darling, darling—! Now Rufus, Aunt Hannah is going to take you down to Grandma Lynch's for the rest of the morning. Mama will come by later, and then we'll go and see Daddy once more, so you can say good-bye to him. *(She kisses him.)* You be very quiet and very good.
RUFUS. How could he have a fatal accident if he wasn't drunk?
MARY. *(Suddenly turning away from him.)* Hannah!

(HANNAH takes RUFUS' hand and they start off Right. MARY turns to look after them until they are off, then quickly goes into the back part of the house.)

RALPH. *(Entering.)* Don't you fret, ev'r'body, I'm

62

goana see us through this grievious day—! (*As the* Two
FAMILIES *come on.*) Get in here, Jim-Wilson, you're
goana spend the afternoon with your cousin Rufus and
you play nice with 'im! Andrew, m' Chalmers is right
out front and I'm goana drive Mary and Paw and Maw
and you follow me with th' others—you all right, Paw?
Try to be brave, Maw, try to be brave—!

JESSIE. Jes' leave me be, Ralph.

RALPH. Cry your heart out, Maw. It's natural at a
time like this. I'm gonna be two sons to you now; I'm
gonna be as many sons as you want.

JESSIE. Jes' leave me be.

RALPH. Well, if anybody needs me, I'll be right outside. (*He goes out and sits in the swing.*)

SALLY. I feel so bad about my dress, Mother Follet.

JESSIE. You look fine, Sally.

SALLY. (*Ashamed.*) I wish it was black.

JESSIE. Imagine bein' young enough not to have a
black dress. Imagine that, Miz Lynch.

CATHERINE. What is it, Joel?

JOEL. *Black dresses.*

CATHERINE. Oh. (*She looks around the room.*) Is anybody speaking?

JOEL. No, Catherine.

CATHERINE. When I was a girl in Michigan, the
dressmaker and the milliner used to come to the house.
They were almost the first to arrive. After the Priest, of
course, but before the undertaker. They filled in that
gap. Nobody ever knew how they *knew* when to come,
for they were never summoned—they just appeared, as if
they had an extra sense about such things. And they
always wore purple to show they weren't *of* the tragedy
but in sympathy to it. (*She looks from one to the other.
They seem to be waiting. She nods and smiles.*) I've
finished.

JESSIE. If a woman has a usual life, one black dress
will see her through it.

CATHERINE. Beg pardon?

JESSIE. (*Sympathetically.*) She really *don't* hear good,
do she?

63

JOEL. (*After a pause.*) In Japan they say white is the color of mourning.

JESSIE. Now, that wouldn't seem right.

JOEL. Black wouldn't seem right to them.

JESSIE. You all right, Paw?

JOHN HENRY. There's Granmaw sittin' up on that mountain for a hundred and three years. And here's me with two attacks to m'credit. And still, Jay's the one that gets took. (*He shakes his head sadly.*) Not Jay. Never Jay.

JESSIE. Now, Paw.

JOHN HENRY. I was all *ready* to go.

(RALPH *sits up in the glider and takes out his bottle as* HANNAH *and* RUFUS *enter Down Right, followed by* MARY *and* FATHER JACKSON. RALPH *quickly hides the bottle and struggles to his feet.*)

RALPH. There he is, the poor little fatherless child.

RUFUS. I saw my daddy, Uncle Ralph.

RALPH. Don't you cry, honey, your Uncle Ralph is here.

MARY. Ralph, I'd like you to meet Father Jackson. This is my brother-in-law, Mr. Follet.

JACKSON. How do you do?

RALPH. How do you do, sir? Can I—take your hat?

JACKSON. (*Taking off his hat.*) Thank you.

HANNAH. That won't be necessary, Father. We're leaving again directly.

RALPH. Was everything all right down to Roberts', Mary? (*To* FATHER JACKSON.) What d' you think of that, sir? With the deceased's only brother an undertaker and willin' to do the generous thing, free of charge, still she puts him in the hands of a stranger. Did y'ever hear of such a thing's that?

JACKSON. It's right for your brother to be buried here, Mr. Follet, where his home was.

RALPH. Now that just plain don't make sense! Jay spent over two-thirds of his life in LaFollette and less'n one-third in Knoxvul! I figgered it out! (*Turning on*

MARY.) You just didn't think of me! You never even thought of me, did yuh?

MARY. No.

RALPH. My own brother! My only brother!

MARY. My own—only husband.

RALPH. All right for you, Mary. (*He stumbles Upstage, taking out his bottle.*) All right for you.

(*He mumbles under his breath. MARY looks at him for a moment, then the procession continues into the living room.*)

CATHERINE. There's little Rufus!

RUFUS. I saw my daddy!

JESSIE. Come to Granmaw, Rufus.

CATHERINE. Come sit on Grandma's lap.

JESSIE. Well, I never!

JOEL. She didn't hear you, Mrs. Follet. No offense.

JESSIE. I keep forgettin'!

JOEL. (*Rising.*) Is it time, Mary?

MARY. Yes, Papa.

SALLY. I'll put Jim-Wilson in Rufus' room for his nap, if that's all right, Mary.

MARY. It's all right, Sally. (SALLY *takes* JIM-WILSON *upstairs.*) Rufus, Mama has to leave you now. You're to be a good boy and stay with Grandma Lynch.

(JOEL *offers his arm to* MARY.)

RALPH. (*In the yard, his mumbling reaching a shout; he smashes his bottle against the back fence.*) I'm glad he's dead!

(MARY *has started to take* JOEL'S *arm. Now she suddenly turns out of the room and into the yard to confront* RALPH.)

MARY. Was he drunk?

HANNAH. (*Following her.*) Mary!

RALPH. On top of ever'thin' else, a priest.

MARY. Was my husband drunk?

RALPH. A Follet in the hands of a priest!

MARY. *Was he drunk!* I have to know. You were with him all afternoon. Tell me!

RALPH. I ain't goana tell yuh, Mary. (*She strikes out at him, but he catches her wrist.*) You thought of me, all right, the night he died, even. And you just didn't want me. I ain't goana tell you nothin'!

HANNAH. We must go, Mary!

RALPH. I ain't goana tell you nothin'!

(MARY *returns to the living room, stands a moment, then goes quickly up to her room.*)

JOEL. (*As* HANNAH *starts up after* MARY.) What's she going to do—?

(HANNAH *gestures silence without stopping. She goes up to find* MARY *in her room.*)

SALLY. (*Running out to* RALPH, *handing him his bowler.*) Are you all right to drive, Ralph—?

RALPH. Well—nobody else is goana drive my Chalmers, let me tell you! (*He goes off, followed by* SALLY.)

HANNAH. Mary, the service is due to start in a very few minutes.

MARY. I'm going to stay here in this room.

HANNAH. Shall I send Father Jackson up to you?

MARY. No.

ANDREW. (*He has come up the stairs.*) Is she coming?

HANNAH. The rest of you get in the cars. We'll come when we can.

(ANDREW *goes back downstairs, and during the following, all but* CATHERINE *and* RUFUS *file out.*)

MARY. Why don't they all leave? You too, Hannah. For I'm not going.

HANNAH. (*Touching her shoulder.*) I'm staying here.

MARY. If you are, please don't touch me. (*In a sudden rage.*) That miserable Ralph! Damn him! You were right, Hannah, God is coming harder to me now. And Jay, too! I can't seem to find either one of them. (HANNAH *stands back quietly.* MARY *gets a necktie from the bureau and scrutinizes the label.*) This necktie was bought in Chattanooga some place. When, do you suppose? Sometimes when he went off like that, he was said to be seen as far as Clairborne County. But Chattanooga — Whatever made Jay do it, *ever!* The night we moved into this house, where did he *go!* And when he first went to work in Papa's office—! (*Stopping, remembering, more softly.*) Not when Rufus was born, though. He was very dearly close to me then, very. But other times, he'd feel himself being closed in, watched by superintendents, he'd say, and— There was always a special quietness about him afterwards, when he came home, as if he were very far away from where he'd been, but very far away from me, too, keeping his distance, but working his way back.

HANNAH. Let the man rest, Mary.

MARY. I want him to rest.

HANNAH. (*Angrily.*) Aren't you even going to attend the funeral!

MARY. Do you think he'll rest simply by lowering him into the ground? I won't watch it. How *can* he when he was *lost* on the very day he died!

HANNAH. You don't know that he was *lost,* or drunk, or *what* he was.

MARY. (*After a moment.*) No. That's just what I don't know.

HANNAH. And *that's* what you can't bear.

MARY. (*After an even longer moment.*) I never knew. Not for sure. There were times we *all* knew about, of course, but there were other times when it wasn't always the whiskey. He'd be gone for a night, or a day, or even two, and I'd know he hadn't touched a drop. And it wasn't any of the other things that come to a woman's mind, either, in case you're thinking that.

HANNAH. I wasn't thinking that.

MARY. Those are easy enemies. It was Market Square. And talking to country people about country secrets that go way on back through the mountains. And any one who'd sing his old songs with him. Or all-night lunch rooms. What's an all-night lunch room for, he'd say, except to sit in all night. And drink coffee so strong it would burn your ribs. And it was locomotives, I suppose, and railroad people, and going fast, and even Charlie Chaplin. What's wrong with Charlie, he'd ask me, not because he didn't know what I'd say, but to make me say it. He's so nasty, I'd say, so vulgar, with his nasty little cane, looking up skirts. And Jay would laugh and go off to see Charlie Chaplin and not come home. Where he went, I can't even imagine, for he'd never tell me. It was always easier to put everything down to whiskey.

HANNAH. To put it down to an enemy.

MARY. Why couldn't I let him have those things, whatever they were, if they meant something to him? Why can't I let him have them now? The dear. He always worked his way back.

ANDREW. (*He runs in, to the foot of the stairs. In a loud whisper.*) Aunt Hannah, we can't wait any longer.

HANNAH. (*At the top.*) All right, Andrew. (ANDREW *goes off again.*)

MARY. They must be suffocating in those cars. (*She smooths the bed for a moment, then straightens up.*) I'm glad Ralph didn't tell me. I must just accept not knowing, mustn't I? I must let Jay *have* what I don't know. (*She picks up her hat and veil and looks at them.*) What if he was drunk? What in the world if he was? Did I honestly think *that* was a gulf? *This* is a gulf! (*She tears a rent in the veil.*) If he was drunk, Hannah, just *if* he was, I hope he loved being. Speeding along in the night—singing at the top of his lungs—racing because he loved to go fast—racing to us because he loved us. And for the time, enjoying—revelling in a freedom that was his, that no place or person, that nothing in this world could ever give him or take away from him. Let's hope that's how it was, Hannah, how he looked death itself in the face. In his strength. (*She puts on the hat and pulls the veil over her face, goes down the stairs.* HANNAH *follows her into the yard.*) That's what we'll put on the gravestone, Hannah. In his strength. (*They go off Left.*)

(CATHERINE *comes into the living room, looks to make sure no one is around, sits on the bench at the piano, and carefully opens the keyboard cover. She is silently running her fingers over the keys when* RUFUS *comes into the room and taps her back.*)

RUFUS. Look, Grandma! (*He shows her a drawing he has just made.*)

CATHERINE. Oh, that's very nice. Is it you?

RUFUS. It's a Belgian.

CATHERINE. Isn't he wearing your new cap?

RUFUS. He's an orphan.

CATHERINE. What are all these riches coming down from the sky?

RUFUS. Those are letters and presents from children all over the world because they feel sorry for him.

CATHERINE. Why, some day, Rufus, you may be an artist like your Uncle Andrew. For the time being, of course, I think it would be *polite* for you to *say* you want to go into law, as your grandfather did and as your dear father was doing. Just for a time. That would only be showing *respect*.

(JOEL *and* ANDREW *come into the living room from Up Left.* JOEL *bangs his hat on the end-table.*)

JOEL. Priggish, mealy-mouthed son-of-a-bitch! I tell you, Andrew, it's enough to make a man retch up his soul!

CATHERINE. (*To* ANDREW.) Was it a lovely funeral, dear?

JOEL. That Jackson! *Father* Jackson, as he insists on being called! Not a *word* would he say over Jay's body, let alone read a service! Because he'd never been baptized. A rule of the Church! Some church!

CATHERINE. Andrew, is there something I should be hearing?

ANDREW. Absolutely not, Mama! Come on, Rufus! (*Going around the back of the house, he takes* RUFUS *into the yard where the swing is.*)

JOEL. You come to one simple single act of Christian charity, and what happens! The rules of the Church forbid it! He's not a member of our little club! I only care, mind you, for Mary's sake! (*He sits beside* CATHERINE *on the couch.*)

CATHERINE. Joel, I don't know what you're saying, but I wish you wouldn't say it. Wait until we get home, dear, where what you say won't matter.

JOEL. Good God!

(*At the swing,* ANDREW *lifts* RUFUS *over the back of it and seats him.*)

ANDREW. I tell you, Rufus, if anything ever makes me believe in God, or Life After Death, it'll be what happened this afternoon in Greenwood Cemetery. There were a lot of clouds, but they were blowing fast, so there was lots of sunshine too. Right when they began to lower your father into the ground, into his grave, a cloud came over and there was a shadow just like iron, and a perfectly magnificent butterfly settled on the coffin, just rested there, right over the breast, and stayed there, just barely making his wings breathe like a heart. He stayed there all the way down, Rufus, until it grated against the bottom like a—rowboat. And just when it did, the sun came out just dazzling bright and he flew up and out of that—hole in the ground, straight up into the sky, so high I couldn't even see him any more. Don't you think that's wonderful, Rufus?

RUFUS. Yes, sir.

ANDREW. If there are any such things as miracles, then *that's* surely miraculous. (*Slowly shaking his head, under his breath.*) A damned *miracle.* (*The* FOLLETS *enter the kitchen from Up Center.* SALLY *goes up to* RUFUS' *room to sit by the sleeping* JIM-WILSON. JESSIE *and* JOHN HENRY *sit at the kitchen table, he in the Left chair.* RALPH *enters just as* MARY *and* HANNAH *come in Down Left. When he sees* MARY, *he takes refuge in the bathroom.* HANNAH *goes upstairs while* MARY *stops in the living room to speak to her* FATHER.)

MARY. (*Lifting her veil back.*) So many people there,

70

Papa, did you notice? I didn't know half of them. We don't always realize, do we, how many others love the people we love. (*She goes upstairs, removes her hat and looks at herself in the mirror.*) Rufus says my face looks like my best china tea-cup. You know, Hannah, the one Jay mended for me so many times. He's beginning to say things like that now, and I don't know where he gets them. (*She starts to put the hat away, but stops.*) People fall away from us, and in time, others grow away from us. That is simply what living is, isn't it? (*She puts the hat on the bureau.*)

HANNAH. (*Now sitting on the bed.*) Why don't you rest?

MARY. You're the one, you haven't stopped for three days.

HANNAH. I'm not tired.

MARY. You must be dead—the words that come to mind.

HANNAH. Not dead. Older perhaps. I'm content to be.

MARY. Well, you're going to lie down for just a minute.

HANNAH. There's supper to be fixed for that mob.

MARY. Not yet.

HANNAH. Perhaps just for a moment. (*She lies down.*)

MARY. Hannah, I love and revere everyone in this world who has ever suffered. I truly do, even those who have failed to endure.

HANNAH. I like the way you call me Hannah now, instead of Aunt Hannah.

MARY. We're that much closer.

HANNAH. Will you let me know when it's time to get started again?

MARY. I'll let you know.

(*She takes* HANNAH's *glasses off, puts them on the bureau, looks in on* SALLY *and* JIM-WILSON *in* RUFUS' *room. During this,* RALPH *comes out of the bathroom, goes into the kitchen yard and Offstage Up Right.*)

SALLY. He sleeps too much, Mary. He just sleeps and sleeps.

MARY. (*She leaves them, stops in front of the stairs as if looking out of upstairs hall window.*) Be with us all you can, my darling, my dearest. This is good-bye.

(*During the following* CATHERINE-JOEL *scene,* MARY *comes down the stairs, takes the portrait of* JAY *from the hall closet.*)

CATHERINE. I quite agree with you, Joel.

JOEL. I didn't say anything.

CATHERINE. Somebody did.

JOEL. What did they say?

CATHERINE. (*Primly.*) They said how fortunate we have been, you and I, to have lived so many years without losing each other.

JOEL. I did say it.

CATHERINE. I must have been mistaken.

JOEL. You weren't mistaken, Catherine. That's—what —I—said!

CATHERINE. (*Patting his hand several times.*) Never mind, dear.

(JOEL *and* CATHERINE *watch* MARY *as she enters with* JAY's *portrait, but she seems unaware of their presence. She places it on the music rack of the piano, steps back and gazes at the picture.*)

JESSIE. How's your breath, Paw?

JOHN HENRY. Pretty fair.

(MARY *squeezes* JOEL's *hand, touches* CATHERINE's *cheek, goes into the kitchen where* JESSIE *and* JOHN HENRY *are sitting. She kisses his forehead and the top of* JESSIE's *head, then goes out into the yard where she hugs* ANDREW.)

MARY. You can actually *feel* summer coming on.

ANDREW. At last.

MARY. There's just one more thing, Andrew. Would you keep an eye on Ralph for the rest of the day? (ANDREW *groans.*) He has to drive his family back to

LaFollette tonight, and goodness sakes, we don't want any accidents. (ANDREW *goes off Up Right to hunt for* RALPH. MARY *sits on the swing beside* RUFUS.) My, you can see all the way to North Knoxville.

RUFUS. Mama?

MARY. Yes?

RUFUS. We sur—sur—

MARY. What are you trying to say?

RUFUS. We sur—*vived*, didn't we, Mama?

MARY. Why yes, darling, we survived.

RUFUS. Am I a norphan now?

MARY. An *orphan*—?

RUFUS. Like the Belgians?

MARY. Of *course* you're not an orphan, Rufus. Orphans haven't got *either* a father or a mother.

RUFUS. Am I half a norphan then?

MARY. Rufus, orphans don't have anybody to love them or take care of them, and you *do!* Oh darling, Mama's wanted to see more of you these last days, a lot more. But you do know how much she loves you, with all her heart and soul, all her life—you know that, don't you?

RUFUS. Will we still get the surprise, Mama?

MARY. I promised you, didn't I? Did you ever know me to break a promise? (*He shakes his head. They get up from the swing.*) Well then, the surprise will come, just as I said. And do you want to know what it's going to be, Rufus?

RUFUS. (*Eagerly.*) What?

MARY. A baby. (*He considers this, not too enthusiastically, and looks down at the ground.*) You're going to have a baby sister. Or it may turn out to be a brother, but I dearly hope it will be a sister. Isn't that wonderful?

RUFUS. (*Figuring it through.*) If I'm half a norphan, Mama, then the baby will be half a norphan, and the two of us together will be a *whole* norphan.

MARY. (*Impatiently.*) Rufus, you're to stop *wanting* to be an *orphan!* Goodness sakes! You be thankful you're not! They sound lucky to you because they're far

73

away and everybody talks about them right now. But they're very, very unhappy little children. Do you hear?

RUFUS. Yes, Mama. (*Retaining, however, a few private hopes.*) Why can't we get the baby right away?

MARY. The time will pass more quickly than you think, much more quickly. And when it does—when she does come to us, you must help her all you can.

RUFUS. Why?

MARY. Because she'll be just beginning. She'll have so much to learn, and I'm counting on you to teach her, because you're so much older and have had so much more experience. She'll be very small and lost, you see, and very delicate.

RUFUS. Like a butterfly?

MARY. (*Somewhat mystified.*) Why, that's a very beautiful thought, Rufus, a very grown-up way to put it.

RUFUS. (*Excitedly.*) Look Mama, there's a train crossing the viaduck!

MARY. It's time to go home, darling.

RUFUS. Let's just watch that train go by. (*He watches excitedly. She looks off, not in the same direction. Pointing at the train, he slowly walks Right and sings "Get on board little children."*) Where's the baby now, Mama?

MARY. Up in Heaven— (*She changes her mind, walks towards him and puts her hand to her waist.*) Right here. (*She takes his hand and places it on her waist.*) Yes, darling. Right here. (*She kneels down to him and holds him by the shoulders.*) You see, Rufus, when a grown man and woman love each other, truly love each other, as Daddy and Mother did, then they get married, and that's the beginning of a family. (*The LIGHTS are now up full on the house with all the* FOLLETS *and* LYNCHES *in the various rooms.* MARY *turns Upstage and leads* RUFUS *home as the CURTAIN begins to fall.*) It will happen to you one day, before you know it, so I want you to listen very carefully to everything I'm going to tell you because I think it's time you knew about it, and I want you to ask questions if you don't understand. Will you do that, darling?

THE CURTAIN IS DOWN

OLD GREY GOOSE

(Aunt Rhodie)

Go tell Aunt Rhodie, Go tell Aunt Rhodie,
Go tell Aunt Rhodie that the old grey goose is dead.

One she's been savin', the one she's been savin',
Yes, the one she's been savin' to make a feather bed.

Old gander's weepin', the old gander's weepin',
Oh, the old gander's weepin' because his wife is dead.

The goslins are mournin', the goslins are mournin',
The goslins are mournin', because their mother's dead.

She died in the mill-pond, she died in the mill-pond,
She died in the mill-pond from standin' on her head.

Go tell Aunt Rhodie, oh, go tell Aunt Rhodie,
Oh, go tell Aunt Rhodie the old grey goose is dead.

SUGAR BABE

Every time the sun goes down,
'Nother dollar made for Betsy Brown.
—Sugar Babe.

There's a good old saying, Lord, everybody know
You can't track a rabbit when there ain't no snow.
—Sugar Babe.

Now it ain't going to rain and it ain't going to snow
The sun's going to shine and the wind's going to blow.
—Sugar Babe.

PROPERTY PLOT

ACT ONE

Kitchen
Table (Pedestal)
2 Chairs
1 Stool
1 Cupboard
1 Stove (Gas)
1 Ice box
1 Sink (practical)
2 Shelves (above sink)
1 Change room

On Table
Oilcloth
Picnic hamper

On Cupboard
Telephone (stand-up kind)

In Cupboard
6 Spoons in drawer
1 Cup and saucer (1)
2 Cups and saucers (2)
1 Sugar bowl w/spoon (2)
1 Box of zuzus (2)

On Stove
1 Coffee pot w/coke (1)
1 Tea kettle w/water (2)
1 Box of kitchen matches
1 Cannister of coffee (brown sugar)
1 Cannister of tea (cut rope)
1 Strainer in tea cannister
1 Spoon in coffee cannister
1 Ash tray
1 Pot holder

On Ice Box
1 Tray w/doily and 7 glasses
1 Small towel over glasses

In Ice Box
1 Pitcher of lemonade
1 Small pitcher of milk (2)

On Sink
1 Towel rack w/2 towels
1 Soap dish w/soap

Under Sink
1 Trash can (padded)

On Shelves Above Sink
6 Glasses (2)
1 Water pitcher w/water (2)
1 Vase of flowers (1, 2)

In Change Room
1 Water tank
1 Drain pan
1 Bottle of Smelling Salts
1 Nightgown (costume—Mary's)
1 Nightgown and slippers and gaudy cap (costume—Rufus')
2 Vases of flowers (2)

Hall
Closet
Bench

In Closet
1 Whiskey bottle w/cork (1, 2)

Living Room
Sofa
Sofa table
End table
Morris chair
Straight chair
Piano
Piano bench

On Sofa
2 Bolsters
2 Pillows

On Sofa Table
1 Cloth runner
1 Lamp
1 Coloring book w/crayons
1 Book of classical piano music
(Pre-set on bottom shelf)

76

On Morris Chair
1 Shot bottom ash tray
On Piano (Closed)
1 Cloth runner
1 Clock (set at 11:30)
1 Pipe rack w/5 pipes
1 Tobacco pouch w/tobacco
1 Box of matches
1 Pipe scraper
Mary's Room
Bed
Bureau
Chair
Window shade *(up)*
On Bed
Mattress
2 Sheets
1 Blanket
1 Spread
2 Pillows w/cases
On Bureau
1 Cloth runner
1 Hairbrush
1 Rosary
Mary's robe (U. S. side of
bureau)
5 Ties (on hook, D. S. side
of bureau)
Rufus' Room
Bed
Rocking chair
Blanket chest
2 Window shades *(down)*
On Bed
Mattress
2 Sheets
1 Blanket
1 Spread
1 Pillow w/case
Rufus' knickers (costume)
On Top Step
1 Cloth dog (ear easily re-
moved)

Off Right
1 Briefcase (Jay)
2 Law books (Jay)
1 Pocket watch (Jay)
1 Pipe (Jay)
1 Pipe scraper (Jay)
1 Handkerchief (Jay)
1 Box of matches (Jay)
1 Wheel chair w/blanket
1 Bag of candy (Hannah)
1 Change purse w/2 nickels
(Hannah)
1 Bible w/rosary (Fr. Jackson)
2 Sets of books w/straps
(Boys)
1 Apron (Hannah 2nd act
costume)
Off Left
1 Pint Flask (¼ full, Ralph)
1 Handkerchief (Ralph)
1 Calling card (Ralph)
1 Inner tube (Jessie)
1 Pocket watch (Joel)
1 "New Republic" Magazine
(Joel)
1 Picture of "Jay"—wrapped
(for 2nd act)
1 Piece of material (for 2nd
act)
1 Ear trumpet (for 2nd act)
1 Newspaper (for 3rd act)
1 Kid's boat
Up Center
1 Quilt (Andrew)
1 Breakable whiskey flask
(Ralph)
1 Sketch book w/crayon
(Rufus)
1 Boy's school satchel
(Rufus)

Strike
Bench
Straight chair
Tray w/glasses and towel
Pitcher of lemonade
Cup and saucer from piano
Whiskey flask from trash can
Briefcase, satchel, coloring book, crayons
Mary's dress from change room
Rufus' knickers from his bedroom

Move
Kitchen table, chairs, stool to new positions
Sofa, sofa table, end table, Morris chair to new positions
Piano and piano bench to new positions
Open piano
Rufus' bed, rocking chair to new positions
Make beds
Straighten towels on towel rack
Clean up kitchen

Set
Picture of "Jay" behind sofa
Classical music open on piano
Ash tray on piano
Curtain material on sofa
Ear trumpet on kitchen table
Clock to 10:25   N.B.

Check
Telephone on cupboard
2 Cups and saucers in cupboard
1 Sugar bowl w/spoon in cupboard
1 Box of zuzus in cupboard
Tea strainer in tea cannister
Box of matches and pot holder
Milk pitcher in ice box
Bottle of whiskey in closet
Glasses and water pitcher on shelf
Rufus' shade *(down)*
Mary's shade *(up)*

Off Right
Bag of candy
Change purse and 2 nickels

Off Left
"New Republic"
Kid's boat

Up Center
Quilt
Rufus—hat and handkerchief
Hannah—purse

ACT THREE

Strike
All flowers
Bottle of whiskey
Used glasses
Water pitcher
Cups and saucers from kitchen table
Box of zuzus and sugar bowl to cupboard
Tea kettle and pot holder to stove
Music from piano

Move
Kitchen chairs out from table
Sofa, table, end table, Morris chair to new positions
Close piano
Ash tray from piano to arm of Morris chair
All blinds *(down)*

Set
Newspaper on sofa
Rosary on head board of Mary's bed
Make Rufus' bed
Gaudy cap on Rufus' bed (Costume)
Mary's hat and veil on sofa table

Check
Picture of "Jay" in closet

Off Right
Bible and rosary (Father Jackson)
4 Sets of books (Boys)

Off Left
Inner tube (Jessie)

Up Center
Breakable whiskey flask
Sketch book w/crayon

COSTUME PLOT

WOMEN

MARY

ACT ONE

1. Dress—Pale green challis skirt with lighter green long-sleeved blouse; petticoat, beige; stockings, black; shoes, black
   (Quick change—on stage)
2. Nightgown—off-white muslin with high neck; wrapper, blue print flannelette with belt; slippers

ACT TWO

1. Dress—Burgundy wool with shirt-waist sleeves, self-color banded trim; petticoat, beige; stockings, black; shoes, black

ACT THREE

1. REPEAT of nightgown, wrapper and slippers
   (Two minute change—off)
2. Dress—black wool with gored skirt, high-necked black dickey; petticoat, black; stockings, black; shoes, black; hat, black straw; veil, black chiffon w/crepe edge

AUNT HANNAH

ACT TWO

1. Skirt—blue; blouse, natural silk; petticoat, beige; coat, light blue wool ¾; hat, black straw, blue flower; purse; stockings, black; shoes, black
   (Quick change—off)
   Remove coat, hat, purse. *Put on* apron, gingham

ACT THREE

1. Skirt, black; blouse, black silk; petticoat, black; jacket, black wool; hat, black straw; veil, black chiffon; stockings, black; shoes, black

CATHERINE

ACT TWO

1. Dress, lavender cotton; petticoat, white crepe; stole, white and pale green w/fringe; stockings, black; shoes, black

ACT THREE

1. Dress, black crepe; petticoat, black; coat, black bengaline; hat, black felt; stockings, black; shoes, black

SALLY

ACT ONE

1. Skirt, yellow gabardine; blouse, pink silk, long sleeves; stole, white, knitted, fringed; petticoat, beige cotton; hat, natural straw, flowers; stockings, black; shoes, black

80

2. Dress, blue pin-stripe wool; petticoat, black; hat, black with blue band; stockings, black; shoes, black

JESSIE
ACT ONE
1. Dress, reddish print challis; sweater, dark burgundy; petticoat, tan; stockings, black; shoes, black
ACT THREE
1. Dress, black silk taffeta; shawl, nun's veiling; hat, black taffeta; stockings, black; shoes, black

AUNT SADIE
ACT ONE
1. Dress, dusky rose print; apron, Pillsbury flour-bag; slippers; petticoat, beige

GREAT GRANMAW
ACT ONE
1. Dress, brown print cotton; petticoat, beige; slippers, felt

MEN

RUFUS
ACT ONE
1. Knickers, neutral color; shirt; tie; belt; stockings, black; shoes, black
   (Change—on stage)
2. Another pair of knickers
ACT TWO
1. Jacket, mustard; knickers, dark blue; shirt; tie; belt; stockings, black; shoes, black; hat, grey felt
   (Change—off)
   Remove everything—*Put on* night shirt—off white cap, gaudy plaid
ACT THREE
1. Knickers, same as in Act Two; jacket, blue serge; shirt; tie; belt; stockings, black; shoes, black; cap, blue serge

RALPH
ACT ONE
1. Suit, beige linen; shirt, red and white stripe; tie, gaudy print; belt and suspenders; shoes, brown; stockings, brown
ACT THREE
1. Suit, black business; shirt, white; tie, black; belt; hat, black bowler; stockings, black; shoes, black

JAY

ACT ONE

1. Suit, Harris tweed, brown; vest; shirt; tie; stockings, brown; shoes, brown

JOHN HENRY

ACT ONE

1. Coat, green wool; trousers, baggy; belt and suspenders; shirt, blue chambray; stockings, black; shoes, black

ACT TWO

1. Suit, black; shirt, white; tie, black; hat, black; stockings, black; shoes, black

ANDREW

ACT TWO

1. Jacket, olive corduroy; slacks, grey; belt; shirt, cream; tie, string; stockings, brown; shoes, brown

ACT THREE

1. Suit, black; vest; shirt, white; hat, black bowler; stockings, black; shoes, black

JOEL

ACT TWO

1. Suit, brown tweed; vest; belt; shirt, white; tie; stockings, black; shoes, black

ACT THREE

1. Suit, black; vest; belt; shirt, white; tie, black; hat, black fedora; stockings, black; shoes, black

JIM-WILSON

ACT ONE

1. Suit, beige linen, long pants; shirt, red and white stripe; tie; belt; stockings, black; shoes, black

ACT THREE

1. Suit, grey; shirt; tie; belt; stockings, black; shoes, black

4 BOYS

ACTS ONE, TWO AND THREE

Overalls, shirts, sweaters; knickers, caps, stockings, shoes, sneakers

FATHER JACKSON

ACT THREE

1. Suit, black; vest, priest's black dickey; collar, clerical; hat, black felt; stockings, black; shoes, black

FIRST BOY

ACT ONE

1. Sneakers; stockings, black; knickers, dark brown; shirt, red and blue check; sweater, light blue V-neck; cap, purple striped visor cap

ACT TWO

1. Change blue sweater to green.
   Everything else remains same

ACT THREE

1. Sneakers, stockings, knickers—same; white shirt and tie; taupe shaded wool jacket

SECOND BOY

ACT ONE

1. Sneakers; stockings, black; knickers, Donegal tweed; shirt, dark green; vest, light grey, open; cap, red, pink and grey checkered

ACT TWO

1. Put on blue overalls instead of knickers
   Change shirt to brown checked

ACT THREE

1. Put knickers back on

THIRD BOY

ACT ONE

1. Shoes, brown; stockings, black; knickers, olive corduroy; shirt, yellow; sweater, red; jacket, brown tweed; cap, grey wool w/short visor

ACT TWO

1. Knickers, grey and white checked; jacket, same; no sweater

ACT THREE

1. Knickers, same; shirt, same; tie; no sweater; shoes, stockings, cap, jacket, same

FOURTH BOY

ACT ONE

1. Sneakers, black stockings; knickers, dark blue; sweater, yellow turtle neck; jacket, electric blue; beanie, grey suede

ACT TWO

1. Change to long light blue trousers; dark blue turtle neck sweater; no jacket

ACT THREE

1. Put on jacket

COSTUME PRE-SETS AND CLEARING

ACT ONE

Pre-Set

> Mary's nightgown—in change room
> Mary's slippers—in change room
> Rufus' gaudy cap—in change room
> Rufus' nightgown—in change room
> Rufus' knickers (beige)—in Rufus' room
> Mary's wrapper—in Mary's room

FIRST INTERMISSION

Strike

> Mary's dress, petticoat
> Shoes, stockings—from change room
> Rufus' knickers—from Rufus' room

ACT TWO

Pre-Set

> Rufus' hat—in Rufus' room
> Rufus' handkerchief—in Rufus' room
> Hannah's apron—off Center

During Act

> Take off Hannah's coat, hat, purse (she exits R.)
> Put on Hannah's apron

SECOND INTERMISSION

Strike

> Rufus' shoes, stockings, coat, hat, knickers—from change room

ACT THREE

Pre-Set

> Rufus' gaudy cap on his head
> Mary's hat and veil on table back of sofa in living room

UPPER PLATFORM

"ALL THE WAY HOME"

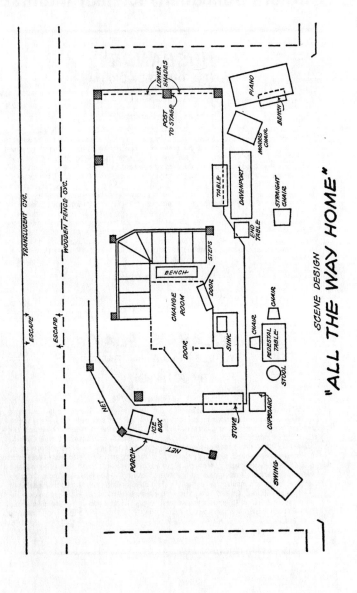

SCENE DESIGN

"ALL THE WAY HOME"

HUSBANDRY

(LITTLE THEATRE—DRAMA)

By PATRICK TOVATT

2 men, 2 women—Interior

At its recent world premiere at the famed Actors Theatre of Louisville, this enticing new drama moved an audience of theatre professionals up off their seats and on to their feet to cheer. Mr. Tovatt has given us an insightful drama about what is happening to the small, family farm in America—and what this means for the future of the country. The scene is a farmhouse whose owners are on the verge of losing their farm. They are visited by their son and his wife, who live "only" eight hours' drive away. The son has a good job in the city, and his wife does, too. The son, Harry, is really put on the horns of a dilemma when he realizes that he is his folks' only hope. The old man can't go it alone anymore—and he needs his son. Pulling at him from the other side is his wife, who does not want to leave her job and uproot her family to become a farm wife. *Husbandry*, then, is ultimately about what it means to be a *husband*—both in the farm and in the family sense. *Variety* praised the "delicacy of Tovatt's dialogue", and called the play "a literate exploration of family responsibilities in a mobile society." Said *Time*: "The play simmers so gently for so long, as each potential confrontation is deflected with Chekhovian shrugs and silences, that when it boils into hostility it sears the audience." (#10169)

(Royalty, $60–$40.)

CLARA'S PLAY

(LITTLE THEATRE—DRAMA)

By JOHN OLIVE

3 men, 1 woman—Exterior

Clara, an aging spinster, lives alone in a remote farmhouse. She is the last surviving member of one of the area's most prominent families. It is summer, 1915. Enter an immigrant, feisty soul named Sverre looking for a few days' work before moving on. But Clara's farm needs more than just a few days' work, and Sverre stays on to help Clara fix up and run the farm. It soon becomes clear unscrupulous local businessmen are bilking Clara out of money and hope to gain control of her property. Sverre agrees to stay on to help Clara keep her family's property. "A story of determination, loyalty. It has more than a measure of love, of resignation, of humor and loyalty."—Chicago Sun-Times. "A playwright of unusual sensitivity in delineating character and exploring human relationships." —Chicago Tribune. "Gracefully-written, with a real sense of place."—Village Voice. A recent success both at Chicago's fine Wisdom Bridge Theatre and at the Great American Play Festival of the world-reknowned Actors Theatre of Louisville; and, on tour, starring Jean Stapleton. (#5076)

(Royalty, $50–$35.)